ENGLISH EXPRESSO

2 주제편

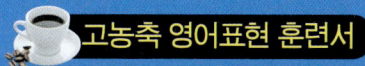
고농축 영어표현 훈련서

잉글리시 엑스프레소

윤주영 지음

Hi English

잉글리시 엑스프레소 주제편

지은이	윤주영
펴낸이	윤주영
펴낸곳	HiEnglish
펴낸날	2015년 11월 30일 초판 1쇄 발행
전화	(02) 335 1002
팩스	(02) 6499 0219
주소	서울 마포구 홍익로5안길 8
홈페이지	www.hienglish.com
이메일	editor1@hienglish.com
등록번호	제2005-000040호
ISBN	979-11-85342-19-1
	979-11-85342-17-7(set)
Copyright	ⓒ 2015 HiEnglish
정가	16,800원
참여한 사람들	장진경, Josh Lee, 윤정현, 손보름, 서정민, 이윤정, Bruce Alexander Grant

All rights reserved. No part of this publication may be reproduced, stored in a retrieval system, or transmitted in any form or by any means, electronic, mechanical, photocopying, recording, or otherwise, without the prior permission of the publisher.

PREFACE

왜 영어가 안 될까요?

우리말에 딱맞는 영어 표현이 안 떠올라 꿀 먹은 벙어리가 된 경험 다들 해보셨나요? 하얘진 머리 속을 뒤로 하고 용기 내어 우리말을 한 단어 한 단어 영어로 바꿔 말해보지만 결국 아무도 알아듣지 못하는 희한한 외계어가 탄생합니다.

모두 굳어진 모국어 언어 체계가 가져온 모국어 간섭 현상 때문입니다. 성인 학습자가 영어로 말할 때는 머리 속에서 한국말 언어 체계를 가동시키기 때문에, 영어 표현도 한국말로 자주 쓰는 표현과 의미적으로 대응하는 표현 중심으로 알아두는 것이 좋습니다. 이때 덩어리째 입력하고 바로 출력될 수 있게 하는 것이 중요한데, 그 때 그 때 단어 단위로 말을 짜 맞추어서는 유창성과 정확성을 기대하기 어렵기 때문입니다.

따라서 평상시에 영어 문장을 먼저 보고 그것의 한글 번역을 확인하는 것보다는 한국어를 먼저 본 후 영어 대응 표현을 확인하는 것이 더 효과적이라고 할 수 있겠습니다. 실제로 성인이 영어로 대화할 때 머리 속에서 일어나는 복잡한 과정을 가장 유사하게 재연하기 때문입니다.

본 교재는 굳어진 언어체계를 가진 성인 학습자의 모국어인 한국어를 학습 매개체로 적극 활용하였습니다. 동시에 영어를 제 2언어(English as a second language)가 아니라 외국어(English as a foreign language)로 학습해야 하는 한국 학습자에게 반드시 필요한 반복 훈련이 용이하도록 구성하였습니다. 이 책이 제시하는 학습 전략과 핵심 표현들을 따라가다 보면 그 동안 수많은 시행착오를 거쳤던 한국의 영어 학습자들의 어려움을 상당 부분 해결할 수 있으리라 자신합니다.

2015년 가을
저자

CONTENTS

Unit 01	**Family** 가족	13
Unit 02	**Weather** 날씨	23
Unit 03	**Television** 텔레비전	33
Unit 04	**Smartphone** 스마트폰	43
Unit 05	**Emotions** 감정	53
Unit 06	**Holiday** 명절	63
Unit 07	**Dress Code** 드레스 코드	73
Unit 08	**Meetings** 회의	83
Unit 09	**Personality** 성격	93
Unit 10	**Drinking** 음주	103

Unit 11	**SNS** SNS	113
Unit 12	**Shopping** 쇼핑	123
Unit 13	**Photos** 사진	133
Unit 14	**Dating** 연애	143
Unit 15	**Lost and Found** 분실물	153
Unit 16	**Appearance** 외모	163
Unit 17	**Mystery** 미스터리	173
Unit 18	**Traveling** 여행	183
Unit 19	**Food** 음식	193
Unit 20	**Sports** 스포츠	203

ABOUT THE BOOK

Dialogue Expressions
대화 상황에서 빈번히 쓰이지만 막상 영어로 말하려면 잘 안 나오는 표현들만 엄선하였습니다. 우리말로 먼저 제시한 후 그것을 영어로 말해볼 수 있도록 구성하였으므로 실제 대화를 시뮬레이션하는 기회가 됩니다.

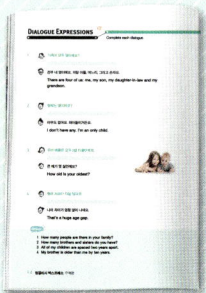

Dialogue Patterns
영어 문장을 스타트시키는 패턴들 중 한국인들이 가장 많이 쓰는 구문을 엄선하여 해당 유닛의 상황 표현들을 결합시켜 제시하였습니다. Chunk 단위 입력으로 인해 유창성 증가에 도움이 됩니다.

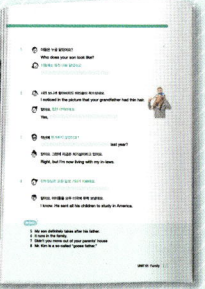

Dialogue Strategy
말의 강도 조절, 했던 말 번복, 맞장구, 다시 되묻기 등의 효과적인 의사소통을 수행하기 위해 기능적으로 필요한 전략 표현들을 학습합니다.

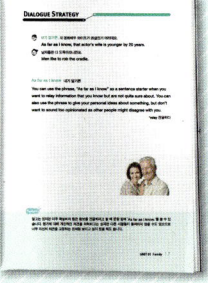

Dialogue Listening
실제 대화 상황이 어떻게 구성되는지 들어볼 수 있습니다. 이해도 체크를 위해 간단한 퀴즈가 제공됩니다. 첫 번째 들을 때는 전반적인 사항을, 두 번째는 세부 정보를 중심으로 들어봅니다.

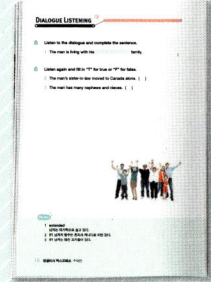

Story Listening

주제와 연관된 흥미로운 이야기들로 구성되어 있습니다. 첫 번째 들을 때는 전반적인 사항을, 두 번째는 세부 정보를 중심으로 들어봅니다. 퀴즈가 끝나면 discussion question으로 토론도 가능합니다.

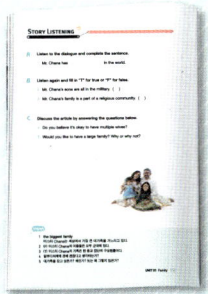

Script

Dialogue Listening과 Story Listening의 Script가 제시됩니다. 이해도 체크를 위한 퀴즈를 모두 풀어본 후 다시 한번 음성파일을 들어보면서 텍스트와 대조해 잘못 들은 부분이 없는지 확인합니다.

Culture Tip

생소한 외국의 문화적 단면을 소개합니다. 우리의 문화와 그들의 문화가 어떻게 다른지를 비교하는 토론 주제로 활용 가능합니다.

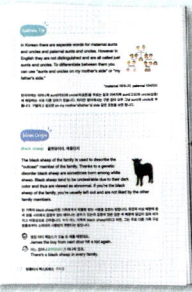

Idiom Origin

표현의 본래적 맥락에서 벗어나 새로운 의미로 사용하게 된 역사적 유래를 되짚어봅니다. 표현을 둘러싼 배경지식과 이미지를 통해 표현의 의미를 각인시키고 대화문 상황을 통해 적절한 활용 예를 학습합니다.

 ENGLISH EXPRESSO

Unit 01 Family

1 가족이 모두 몇이에요?
2 형제는 몇이에요?
3 우리 애들은 모두 2살 터울이에요.
4 형이 저보다 10살 많아요.
5 아들애는 엄마 닮았어요.
6 집안 내력이에요.
7 작년에 분가했어요.
8 김부장님은 요즘 말로 기러기 아빠예요.

1 How many people are there in your family?
2 How many brothers and sisters do you have?
3 All of my children are spaced two years apart.
4 My brother is older than me by ten years.
5 My son takes after his mother.
6 It runs in the family.
7 I moved out of my parents' house last year.
8 Mr. Kim is a so-called "goose father."

Dialogue Expressions

Complete each dialogue.

1   가족이 모두 몇이에요?

     전부 네 명이에요. 저랑 아들, 며느리, 그리고 손자요.
     There are four of us: me, my son, my daughter-in-law and my grandson.

2   형제는 몇이에요?

     아무도 없어요. 외아들이거든요.
     I don't have any. I'm an only child.

3   우리 애들은 모두 2살 터울이에요.

     큰 애가 몇 살인데요?
     How old is your oldest?

4   형이 저보다 10살 많아요.

     나이 차이가 엄청 많이 나네요.
     That's a huge age gap.

Answers

1 How many people are there in your family?
2 How many brothers and sisters do you have?
3 All of my children are spaced two years apart.
4 My brother is older than me by ten years.

5   아들은 누굴 닮았어요?

   Who does your son look like?

   아들애는 완전 아빠 닮았어요.

6   사진 보니까 할아버지도 머리숱이 적으셨네요.

   I noticed in the picture that your grandfather had thin hair.

    맞아요. 집안 내력이에요.

   Yes,

7   작년에 분가하지 않았어요?

   last year?

   맞아요. 그런데 지금은 처가살이하고 있어요.

   Right, but I'm now living with my in-laws.

8   김부장님은 요즘 말로 기러기 아빠예요.

    알아요. 아이들을 모두 미국에 유학 보냈대요.

   I know. He sent all his children to study in America.

   5 My son definitely takes after his father.
   6 it runs in the family.
   7 Didn't you move out of your parents' house
   8 Mr. Kim is a so-called "goose father."

DIALOGUE PATTERNS

Complete each sentence.

A

 어른 모시고 사시나요?
Do you live with your extended family?

 전에는 시부모님과 같이 살았지만 지금은 아니에요.
Well, **I used to** live with my parents-in-law but not anymore.

1 전에는 누나한테 얹혀살았죠.
   I used to _____

2 전에는 혼자 살았어요.
   I used to _____

3 전에는 형제지간에 사이가 좋았죠.
   I used to _____

B

 우리 가족 사진이에요.
This is a photo of my entire family.

 정말 대가족이네요! 20명은 되는 것 같아요.
What a big family! There's like 20 people in there.

4 정말 세상 참 좁네요.
   What a _____

5 정말 우연의 일치네요.
   What a _____

6 이게 웬일이에요!
   What a _____

1 live off my sister.
2 live by myself.
3 get along well with my siblings.
4 small world!
5 coincidence!
6 surprise!

DIALOGUE STRATEGY

 내가 알기론, 저 영화배우 와이프가 20살인가 어리대요.
As far as I know, that actor's wife is younger by 20 years.

 남자들은 다 도둑이라니깐요.
Men like to rob the cradle.

As far as I know 내가 알기론

You can use the phrase, "As far as I know" as a sentence starter when you want to relay information that you know but are not quite sure about. You can also use the phrase to give your personal ideas about something, but don't want to sound too opinionated as other people might disagree with you.

*relay 전달하다

알고는 있지만 아주 확실하지 않은 정보를 전달하려고 할 때 문장 앞에 'As far as I know'를 쓸 수 있습니다. 뭔가에 대해 개인적인 의견을 피력하고는 싶지만 다른 사람들이 동의하지 않을 수도 있으므로 너무 자신의 의견을 고집하는 것처럼 보이고 싶지 않을 때도 씁니다.

Dialogue Listening

A Listen to the dialogue and complete the sentence.

1 The man is living with his ▓▓▓▓▓▓▓▓ family.

B Listen again and fill in "T" for true or "F" for false.

2 The man's sister-in-law moved to Canada alone. (　)

3 The man has many nephews and nieces. (　)

1 extended
   남자는 대가족으로 살고 있다.
2 (F) 남자의 형수는 혼자서 캐나다로 이민 갔다.
3 (F) 남자는 많은 조카들이 있다.

STORY LISTENING

A Listen to the article and complete the sentence.

1 Mr. Chana has _____ in the world.

B Listen again and fill in "T" for true or "F" for false.

2 Mr. Chana's sons are all in the military. (   )

3 Mr. Chana's family is a part of a religious community. (   )

C Discuss the article by answering the questions below.

4 Do you believe it's okay to have multiple wives?

5 Would you like to have a large family? Why or why not?

1 the biggest family
   미스터 Chana는 세상에서 가장 큰 대가족을 거느리고 있다.
2 (F) 미스터 Chana의 아들들은 모두 군대에 있다.
3 (T) 미스터 Chana의 가족은 한 종교 집단의 구성원들이다.
4 일부다처제에 관해 괜찮다고 생각하는가?
5 대가족을 갖고 싶은가? 왜인가? 또는 왜 그렇지 않은가?

Script for Dialogue Listening

Mia	What a big family! How many people are there in your family?
Richard	I have a family of seven. There's my wife, my son, my daughter, my parents, and my paternal grandma.
Mia	Who is the lady next to your wife?
Richard	She's my sister-in-law.
Mia	Does she live with you?
Richard	She used to live with us after my brother passed away, but she moved to Canada last year.
Mia	Where are her children now?
Richard	My nephews and nieces are living with her in Toronto.
Mia	Do you have any cousins?
Richard	I have many cousins because I have ten aunts and uncles.

sister-in-law 형수, 제수, 올케   **pass away** 죽다   **nephew** 남자조카   **niece** 여자조카   **cousin** 사촌

미아	엄청 대가족이네요! 가족이 모두 몇 명이에요?
리차드	일곱 명이에요. 아내와 아들, 딸, 부모님, 그리고 친할머니요.
미아	아내 옆의 여자분은 누구예요?
리차드	형수님이에요.
미아	같이 살아요?
리차드	형이 죽고나서 함께 살았는데, 작년에 캐나다로 이사 갔어요.
미아	아이들은 지금 어디 있어요?
리차드	조카들은 토론토에서 형수와 함께 살고 있어요.
미아	사촌은 있어요?
리차드	고모와 삼촌이 열 명이나 돼서 사촌이 많아요.

SCRIPT FOR STORY LISTENING

The Largest Family on Earth

How many people are there in your family? Well, Ziona Chana from India is the head of the world's biggest family. He has 39 wives, 94 children, 14 daughters-in-law and 33 grandchildren! That is an astonishing 180 people! One of his wives said that this was possible because Mr. Chana is the most handsome man in the village.

Mr. Chana's family lives in a dormitory-like 100-room house. His oldest wife manages the massive family with military discipline. She makes sure all the daily household chores get done. According to another wife, the family gets along very well. Mr. Chana is the head of a religion that allows men to have multiple spouses. He mentions that he is always looking for new wives. He is even willing to travel abroad to meet his next bride!

daughter-in-law 며느리 **grandchildren** 손주 **astonishing** 놀라운 **dormitory-like** 기숙사 같은 **massive** 거대한 **multiple** 다수의 **spouse** 배우자

세상에서 가장 큰 대가족

당신의 가족은 몇 명인가? 인도의 Ziona Chana는 세상에서 가장 큰 대가족의 가장이다. 그는 39명의 아내와, 94명의 자식, 14명의 며느리와 33명의 손주를 거느리고 있다. 총 180명에 달하는 놀라운 숫자이다. 그의 아내 중 한 명은 미스터 Chana가 마을에서 가장 잘 생긴 사람이기에 이것이 가능하다고 말했다.

미스터 Chana의 가족은 100개의 방이 있는 기숙사 같은 집에서 산다. 가장 나이가 많은 아내가 이 거대한 가족을 군율로 다스린다. 그녀는 매일 하고 있는 가사일이 잘 돌아가게끔 한다. 다른 아내 말에 의하면, 가족들은 서로 아주 잘 지낸다고 한다. 미스터 Chana는 남자들이 다수의 아내를 얻는 것을 허락하는 한 종교의 수장이다. 그는 항상 새로운 아내를 찾고 있다고 한다. 심지어 다음 신부를 만나기 위해 해외로도 갈 용의가 있다고 한다!

Culture Tip

In Korean there are separate words for maternal aunts and uncles and paternal aunts and uncles. However in English they are not distinguished and are all called just aunts and uncles. To differentiate between them you can use "aunts and uncles on my mother's side" or "my father's side."

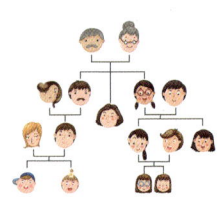

*maternal 어머니의 paternal 아버지의

한국어에는 어머니쪽 aunt(이모)와 uncle(외삼촌)을 부르는 말과 아버지쪽 aunt(고모)와 uncle(삼촌)에 해당하는 서로 다른 단어가 있습니다. 하지만 영어에서는 구분 없이 모두 그냥 aunt와 uncle로 부릅니다. 구별하고 싶으면 on my mother's[father's] side 같은 표현을 쓰면 됩니다.

Idiom Origin

Black sheep 골칫덩어리, 애물단지

The black sheep of the family is used to describe the "outcast" member of the family. Thanks to a genetic disorder black sheep are sometimes born among white sheep. Black sheep tend to be undesirable due to their dark color and thus are viewed as abnormal. If you're the black sheep of the family, you're usually left out and are not liked by the other family members.

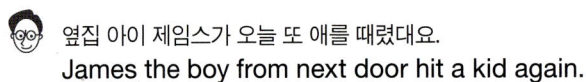

한 가족의 black sheep이란 가족에게서 따돌림 받는 사람을 일컫는 말입니다. 유전적 이상 때문에 흰색 양들 사이에서 검정색 양이 태어나는 경우가 있는데 검정색 양은 검은 색 때문에 달갑지 않게 여겨지고 비정상으로 간주됩니다. 누가 어느 가족의 black sheep이라고 하면, 그는 주로 다른 가족 구성원들로부터 소외되어 사랑받지 못한다는 말입니다.

- 옆집 아이 제임스가 오늘 또 애를 때렸대요.
  James the boy from next door hit a kid again.
- 어느 집이나 골칫덩어리가 하나씩 있죠.
  There's a **black sheep** in every family.

Unit 02 Weather

1 비가 오락가락하네요.
2 황사가 온대요.
3 벚꽃구경 갈래요?
4 정말 덥고 후텁지근하네요.
5 장마가 끝난 거 같아요.
6 어제 열대야 때문에 한숨도 못 잤어요.
7 제가 추위를 많이 타요.
8 대체 몇 겹을 껴입은 거예요?

1 It's raining off and on.
2 A yellow dust storm is coming.
3 Do you want to go view the cherry blossoms?
4 It's really hot and muggy.
5 I think the rainy season is over.
6 I didn't sleep a wink yesterday due to the tropical night.
7 I get chilled easily.
8 How many layers of clothing are you wearing?

Dialogue Expressions

1 밖에 날씨 어때요?
   How's the weather outside?

   비가 오락가락해요. 우산 가져가야 할 것 같아요.
   _____ I think we should take an umbrella.

2 차 위에 저 미세먼지 좀 봐요.
   Look at all the fine dust on the car.

   오늘 마스크 껴야 해요. 황사가 온대요.
   We should wear masks today. _____

3 날씨가 포근하네요.
   The weather is mild today.

   벚꽃구경 갈래요?
   _____

4 정말 덥고 후텁지근하네요.
   _____

   가만히 있어도 땀이 줄줄 흘러요.
   I sweat even when I keep still.

   1 It's raining on and off.
   2 A yellow dust storm is coming.
   3 Do you want to go view the cherry blossoms?
   4 It's really hot and muggy.

5 장마가 끝난 거 같아요.

   이젠 폭염에 대비해야 해요.
   I guess we better get ready for the heat wave now.

6 어제 열대야 때문에 한숨도 못 잤어요.

   전 밤새 선풍기 틀어놓고 잤어요.
   I slept with the fan on the whole night.

7 왜 10월인데 벌써 겨울 옷 입고 있는 거예요?
   Why are you wearing winter clothes in October?

   제가 추위를 많이 타서요.

8 대체 몇 겹을 껴입은 거예요?

   그러게요. 너무 많이 껴입었더니 몸이 둔해요.
   I know. I'm wearing so many that it's hard to move.

Answers

5 I think the rainy season is over.
6 I didn't sleep a wink yesterday due to the tropical night.
7 I get chilled easily.
8 How many layers of clothing are you wearing?

DIALOGUE PATTERNS

Complete each sentence.

A

낮이 점점 길어지고 있어요.
The days **are getting** longer **and** longer.

맞아요. 퇴근하는데 밖이 아직 훤하더라고요.
That's true. I was going home from work and it was still bright.

1 빗줄기가 점점 더 굵어지고 있어요.
                    are getting   **and**

2 날씨가 점점 따뜻해지고 있어요.
                    is getting   **and**

3 상황이 점점 그에게 불리해지고 있어요.
                    are getting   **and**

B

왜 이렇게 늦었어요?
Why are you so late?

길이 미끄러워서 엉금엉금 길 수밖에 없었어요.
The ground was so slippery **I had no choice but to** crawl.

4 비 맞을 수밖에 없었어요.
   I had no choice but to

5 미끄러질 수밖에 없었어요.
   I had no choice but to

6 부채질할 수밖에 없었어요.
   I have no choice but to

1 The raindrops, bigger, bigger.
2 The weather, warmer, warmer.
3 Things, worse, worse for him.
4 get caught in the rain.
5 slip.
6 fan myself.

DIALOGUE STRATEGY

 혹시 모르니까 우산 가져가요.
Take an umbrella with you, **just in case**.

 괜찮을 거 같아요. 일기예보 확인했어요.
I think it will be okay. I checked the weather forecast.

Just in case 혹시 모르니까

"Just in case" is used when there's a possibility of something happening and you should prepare for it. It is usually applied to situations where not preparing has heavy consequences even if the possibility is low. "Just in case" can come either at the front or back of a sentence.

*consequence 결과

'Just in case'는 무언가 일어날 가능성이 있어 그에 대한 준비를 해야 하는 상황에 쓰는 표현으로 가능성이 적더라도 준비하지 않으면 심각한 결과가 생기는 상황에 주로 씁니다. 이 표현은 문장 앞이나 뒤에 모두 올 수 있습니다.

Dialogue Listening

A Listen to the dialogue and complete the sentence.

1 The weather in Seoul is ▓▓▓▓▓▓▓▓

B Listen again and fill in "T" for true or "F" for false.

2 The woman is planning to visit Sydney. (   )

3 The woman recommended that the man bring long-sleeved shirts. (   )

1 hot and rainy.
   서울은 현재 날씨가 덥고 비가 온다.
2 (F) 여자는 시드니를 방문할 예정이다.
3 (T) 여자는 남자에게 긴 소매 셔츠를 가져올 것을 권했다.

STORY LISTENING

A Listen to the article and complete the sentence.

1 Gloomy weather makes us _____ than usual.

B Listen again and fill in "T" for true or "F" for false.

2 Gloomy weather prevents clear thinking. (   )

3 Our minds don't think deeply when we are happy. (   )

C Discuss the article by answering the questions below.

4 Have you ever experienced this yourself?

5 How do different kinds of weather make you feel?

1 remember things better
우울한 날씨는 우리가 평소보다 더 잘 기억할 수 있게 해준다.
2 (F) 우울한 날씨는 명확한 사고를 못하게 만든다.
3 (T) 우리의 정신은 행복할 때 깊이 생각하지 못한다.
4 이러한 경험을 한 적이 있는가?
5 날씨에 따라서 어떤 기분 변화를 느끼는가?

UNIT 02 Weather

● SCRIPT FOR DIALOGUE LISTENING

Sunny   How's the weather over there in Sydney?
Paul   It's been pouring all week. I'd say it's raining cats and dogs but it should be clear soon.
Sunny   Good! So, are you coming to Korea?
Paul   Yes! How's the weather in Seoul now?
Sunny   It will get hotter and hotter because the rainy season will soon be over.
Paul   I see. What's the temperature on a typical day?
Sunny   About 35 degrees Celsius.
Paul   Okay. Should I bring summer clothes?
Sunny   Yes, but bringing a few long-sleeved shirts would be good, too. It can get pretty chilly at night.
Paul   Thanks for the tip.

pour 퍼붓다   raining cats and dogs 비가 억수같이 퍼붓는   be over 끝나다
typical day 일반적인 날   long-sleeved 긴 소매의

써니   그곳 시드니 날씨는 어때요?
폴   이번 주 내내 퍼붓고 있어요. 비가 억수 같이 쏟아진다고 해야겠네요. 그렇지만 곧 날씨가 갤 것 같아요.
써니   좋아요! 그럼, 한국에 올 거예요?
폴   네! 지금 서울 날씨는 어때요?
써니   곧 장마철이 끝나니까 점점 더워질 거예요.
폴   알았어요. 보통 기온이 몇 도예요?
써니   35도 정도요.
폴   좋아요. 여름 옷 가져가면 돼요?
써니   네, 하지만 긴 소매 셔츠 몇 벌 가져오는 것도 좋을 거예요. 밤에는 꽤 쌀쌀하거든요.
폴   좋은 정보 고마워요.

SCRIPT FOR STORY LISTENING

Does Gloomy Weather Make Us Smarter?

   Sunny weather can make everyone feel happier. However, sunny weather isn't always great news. A study conducted by researchers in Australia connected one's memory with the day's weather. Researchers placed ten unusual objects at the check-out counter in a shop in Sydney. They asked shoppers leaving the store to recall all the unusual items they noticed. On rainy days, customers recalled three times as many items as on sunny days.

   Researchers say that gloomy weather makes us think more clearly and deeper than usual. Therefore, it helps us to recall information more accurately. On the other hand, sunny weather uplifts people's moods. This leads to less focus on the details around us. So, if you have a big test coming up, you should hope for rainy weather!

gloomy 우울한   conduct 실행하다   recall 떠올리다   accurately 정확히   uplift 끌어올리다

우울한 날씨가 우리를 더 똑똑하게 만드나?

   화창한 날씨는 모두를 더 행복하게 만든다. 하지만 화창한 날이 언제나 좋은 소식인 것은 아니다. 호주에서 실시한 한 연구는 우리의 기억을 날씨와 연관지어 보았다. 연구원들은 시드니에 있는 한 상점 계산대에 10개의 특이한 물건들을 올려 놓았다. 그들은 상점을 나가는 쇼핑객들에게 특이했다고 생각한 모든 물건들을 상기해보라고 했다. 고객들은 화창한 날보다 비 오는 날에 3배나 많은 물건들을 기억해냈다.

   연구원들은 우울한 날씨는 우리가 평소보다 더 분명하고 깊게 생각할 수 있게 해준다고 한다. 그러므로 우울한 날씨는 우리가 정보를 더 정확하게 상기할 수 있도록 도와준다. 한편, 화창한 날씨는 사람들의 기분을 좋게 만들어 준다. 이것으로 인해 우리 주위에 있는 세부적인 것들에 대해 덜 집중하게 된다. 그러니 만약 중요한 시험을 앞두고 있다면, 비가 오기를 기대해야 할 것이다!

UNIT 02 Weather

Culture Tip

Traditionally British and American gentlemen were expected to offer their umbrella if they met a woman without one in a sudden storm. If she accepted, you would simply give it to her. If she hesitated, you would offer to accompany her to her destination but you were not to open a conversation on the way. Is there such umbrella etiquette in Korea?

전통에 의하면 영국이나 미국 신사들은 갑작스런 폭우에 우산을 들고 있지 않은 여성을 마주치게 될 경우 자신들의 우산을 건네주게 되어 있습니다. 만일 여성이 호의를 받아들이면 우산을 그냥 줍니다. 만일 여성이 받으려 하지 않으면 여성의 목적지까지 동행할 것을 제의할 수 있지만 가는 길에 대화는 할 수 없습니다. 한국에도 이런 우산 에티켓이 있나요?

Idiom Origin

Under the weather 몸이 안 좋다, 컨디션이 좋지 않다

The term "under the weather" comes from the days of old sailing ships when the weather had a profound effect on the health of sailors. Also when the weather was rough, sick sailors were often sent below deck for protection thus they would be "under the weather."

*rough 거친

'Under the weather'라는 말은 범선을 타고 다니던 오래 전 시절로부터 유래되었는데 그때 날씨는 선원들의 건강에 중대한 영향을 미쳤습니다. 날씨가 궂으면 아픈 선원을 보호하려고 갑판 아래로 내려보냈는데 그래서 아픈 선원은 나쁜 날씨 아래에(under the weather) 있게 된 것입니다.

 제드는 오늘 몸이 안 좋은 거예요? 어디에도 안 보이네요.
　　Is Jed **under the weather** today? I don't see him anywhere.

 어제 비 쫄딱 맞더니 결국 자리에 드러누웠어요.
　　Yeah, he is sick in bed after being caught out in the rain yesterday.

Unit 03 Television

1 최고 시청률을 기록했어요.
2 또 출생의 비밀이에요?
3 요즘 먹방이 대세예요.
4 광고만 5분째 하고 있어요.
5 그 드라마 마지막 NG장면 봤어요?
6 이 리얼리티 쇼는 자막이 진짜 웃겨요.
7 예능프로는 결방한대요.
8 '뉴스룸' 몇 번에서 하죠?

1 It recorded the highest viewer ratings.
2 Is it another birth secret?
3 Celebrity food shows are all the rave these days.
4 Commercials have been running for five minutes now.
5 Did you see the last blooper from that TV drama?
6 The captions for this reality show are so funny.
7 Entertainment shows aren't being aired today.
8 What channel is *Newsroom* on?

Dialogue Expressions

Complete each dialogue.

1. 어제 새 주말 드라마 봤어요?
   Did you watch the new weekend soap opera yesterday?

   봤어요. 시작하자마자 최고 시청률을 기록했대요.
   I did. _____ as soon as it premiered.

2. 주인공이 그 집 친딸이란 게 드러났어요.
   The main character was revealed to be that family's real daughter.

   또 출생의 비밀이에요?
   _____

3. 그 셰프가 요즘 TV에 자주 나오더라구요.
   That chef is on TV a lot these days.

   요즘 연예인 먹방이 대세니까요.
   _____

4. 진짜 짜증나요. 광고만 5분째 하고 있어요.
   This is irritating. _____

   시작하면 불러요.
   Let me know when the program is back on.

1. It recorded the highest viewer ratings
2. Is it another birth secret?
3. Celebrity food shows are all the rave these days.
4. Commercials have been running for five minutes now.

5   그 드라마 마지막 NG 장면 봤어요?

　　대사 까먹는데 웃겨 죽는 줄 알았어요.
　　Yeah, I laughed myself to death when he forgot his lines.

6   이 리얼리티 쇼는 자막이 진짜 웃겨요.

　　맞아요. 도대체 작가가 누구예요?
　　I know. Who writes these?

7   오늘 토요일인데 왜 '무한도전' 안 하지?
　　It's Saturday. Why isn't *Infinite Challenge* on today?

　　오늘 모든 예능프로는 결방한대요.

8   손석희 나오는 '뉴스룸' 몇 번에서 하죠?

　　JTBC였던 거 같은데. 18번 틀어봐요.
　　I think it's on JTBC. Turn to channel 18.

Answers

5 Did you see the last blooper from that TV drama?
6 I think the captions for this reality show are so funny.
7 All the entertainment shows aren't being aired today.
8 What channel is *Newsroom* with Sohn Suk-hee on?

DIALOGUE PATTERNS

Complete each sentence.

A 마지막에 둘이 다시 만나게 되요?
Do the two meet again at the end?

 모르는 게 나아요.
You're better off not knowing.

1 재방송[본방송] 보는 게 나아요.
You're better off _____

2 편성표 확인하는 게 나아요.
You're better off _____

3 이게 오히려 더 잘됐어요.
You're better off _____

B 얼굴만 잘 생기면 뭐해요? 발연기인데.
What's the point of good looks if you can't act?

 그래도 광고는 엄청 찍었더라고요.
Still, she filmed so many ads.

4 화면이 이렇게 작은데 모니터 화질만 좋으면 뭐해요?
What's the point of _____

5 친구 많아 봐야 무슨 소용 있어요?
What's the point of _____

6 이제 와서 잘잘못을 따지는 게 무슨 소용이에요?
What's the point of _____

1 watching a rerun [the original airing].
2 checking the TV schedule.
3 this way.
4 having great picture quality on such a small screen?
5 having tons of friends?
6 placing blame at this point?

DIALOGUE STRATEGY

 '선덕여왕' 정말 재밌지 않았어요?
Wasn't *Queen Seondeok* really good?

 실은, 전 사극은 별로예요.
The thing is, I'm not into historical dramas.

The thing is 실은

The phrase "The thing is" is used to offer an explanation, reasoning or fact. It usually comes at the beginning of the sentence with the explanation coming right after it. It is commonly used when one has to summarize something or is questioned about an important issue.

*reasoning 추론

'The thing is'는 설명을 해주거나, 추론 혹은 사실 등을 말할 때 씁니다. 주로 설명을 나타내는 문장 앞부분에 오는데 대개 요약하거나 중요한 것에 대한 질문을 받았을 때 사용됩니다.

Dialogue Listening

A Listen to the dialogue and complete the sentence.

1 The woman is recommending _____ for the man to watch.

B Listen again and fill in "T" for true or "F" for false.

2 The program the woman is talking about is about mysteries. (　)

3 According to the woman the show features good acting. (　)

1　a TV program
　　여자는 남자가 볼 TV 프로그램을 추천하고 있다.
2　(F) 여자가 말하는 프로그램은 미스터리물이다.
3　(T) 여자 말에 따르면 그 프로그램은 훌륭한 연기가 특징이다.

Story Listening

A Listen to the article and complete the sentence.

1 A soccer player was kidnapped as a part of

B Listen again and fill in "T" for true or "F" for false.

2 Bougherra was kidnapped but saved from execution. (   )

3 Bougherra had an argument with a friend in the café. (   )

C Discuss the article by answering the questions below.

4 Do you think the TV show took the prank too far?

5 If you were Bougherra, how would you have reacted to the prank?

1 a TV prank.
   한 축구 선수는 TV 몰래 카메라의 일부로 납치된 것이었다.
2 (F) Bougherra는 납치되었지만 처형되지는 않았다.
3 (F) Bougherra는 카페에서 그의 친구와 말다툼이 있었다.
4 그 TV 쇼는 장난이 너무 지나쳤다고 생각하는가?
5 자신이 Bougherra라면, 이 장난에 어떻게 반응했겠는가?

● SCRIPT FOR DIALOGUE LISTENING

Ted	Any good programs on TV these days?
Kimmy	There's one sitcom I enjoy watching called *Modern Family*.
Ted	What's it about?
Kimmy	It's a family sitcom featuring stories about three families.
Ted	What's so good about it?
Kimmy	Well, first of all, the acting and writing are really good.
Ted	Is it funny?
Kimmy	It's hilarious. I laugh myself sick every time I watch it.
Ted	Really? I better check it out. Thanks for the recommendation.
Kimmy	Glad to help. It's also a good show to watch if you want to learn English.

feature 특징을 이루다   hilarious 아주 우스운

테드	요새 TV 프로그램 재미있는 것 있어요?
키미	내가 잘 보는 '모던 패밀리'라는 게 있어요.
테드	무슨 내용이에요?
키미	세 가족의 살아가는 이야기를 다룬 패밀리 시트콤이에요.
테드	뭐가 재미있는데요?
키미	먼저 연기와 대본이 진짜 좋아요.
테드	웃겨요?
키미	무지 웃겨요. 볼 때마다 웃겨 죽어요.
테드	정말요? 직접 봐야겠네요. 추천해줘서 고마워요.
키미	도울 수 있어서 기뻐요. 영어 배울 때도 보기 좋은 프로예요.

● SCRIPT FOR STORY LISTENING

A Soccer Player's Near Death Experience

Madjid Bougherra is a soccer player who once played for the English Football League. One day he was relaxing at a café with a friend near his hometown in Algeria. Suddenly terrorists burst in and rushed him to a van at gunpoint. Bougherra was blindfolded and driven into the desert. He was forced to kneel in the sand, and feared he would be executed. At that point, the whole thing was revealed to be a prank, to Bougherra's surprise and relief.

The prank was organized by a local TV show. After the episode was broadcast, viewers had mixed opinions. Some thought it was a fun, harmless prank. Others however, expressed concern that the show didn't make the terror threats Algeria is suffering from seem serious.

burst in 불쑥 들어가다　at gunpoint 총을 들이대고　blindfolded 눈을 가린 채　kneel 무릎 꿇다　execute 처형하다　prank 못된 장난　concern 우려　threat 위협

한 축구 선수의 죽을 뻔한 경험

Madjid Bougherra는 한때 영국 축구 리그에서 뛰었던 축구 선수이다. 어느 날 그는 알제리에 있는 그의 고향 근처에서 친구와 함께 한 카페에서 쉬고 있었다. 갑자기 테러범들이 불쑥 나타나 총을 들이대고 차에 태웠다. Bougherra는 눈이 가려진 채 사막으로 끌려 갔다. 그는 모래 위에 강제로 무릎을 꿇은 채 처형될지도 모른다는 두려움에 떨고 있었다. 바로 그때 이 모든 것이 장난이라는 것이 밝혀졌고, Bougherra는 깜짝 놀랐지만 안심할 수 있었다.

이 장난은 한 지역 TV 쇼가 꾸몄다. 이 에피소드가 방송이 된 후, 시청자들은 각기 다른 반응을 보였다. 일부는 이것이 재미있고, 피해가 없는 장난이라고 생각했다. 하지만 다른 일부는 이 쇼가 알제리가 처한 테러의 위협을 대수롭지 않게 만들었다는 우려를 표명했다.

Culture Tip

In America, reality TV and game shows have become a fixture in television after gaining popularity in the early 2000s. Reality TV is especially notable for its unscripted real-life situations, drama, and personal conflicts. What kinds of TV programs are popular in Korea?

*fixture 정착물, 붙박이

미국에서 리얼리티 TV와 게임쇼는 2000년대 초에 인기를 얻은 후 TV의 고정물이 되어가고 있습니다. 리얼리티 TV는 특히 대본이 없는 실제 상황이나 드라마 그리고 개인적인 갈등을 다루는 것으로 유명합니다. 한국에는 어떤 종류의 TV 프로그램들이 인기가 있나요?

Idiom Origin

Jump on the bandwagon 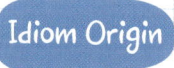 시류에 편승하다, 우세한 쪽에 붙다

When you jump on the bandwagon, you temporarily support and favor a short-lived trend because it is popular at the time. The term originated from decorated bandwagons used by circus workers in order to attract people to the circus. Due to its fleeting nature, "jump on the bandwagon" has a negative tone when used.

*bandwagon 서커스의 악대차 fleeting 순식간에 지나가는

Bandwagon에 뛰어든다는 말은 당시의 인기 때문에 잠깐 유행하는 트렌드를 일시적으로 지지하거나 선호하는 것입니다. 이 표현은 서커스단이 사람들을 끌어 모으려고 사용했던 장식 달린 bandwagon에서 유래되었습니다. 순식간에 지나가버리는 특성으로 인해 'jump on the bandwagon'에는 부정적 뉘앙스가 있습니다.

 방송국들이 시류에 편승해서 리얼리티 TV 쇼를 만들고 있어요.
Broadcasting stations are jumping on the bandwagon and making reality TV shows.

 그러게요. 하도 많아서 기억도 못하겠어요.
I know. There are so many I can't even keep track.

Smartphone

1 진동모드로 해놨어요.
2 여기 와이파이가 안 돼요.
3 광고 전화였어요.
4 문자로 보내줄게요.
5 그 사람이 계속 내 문자를 씹어요.
6 이따 전화할게요.
7 배터리가 얼마 안 남았어요.
8 아까 전화했는데 안 받으시던데요.

1 I put it on vibrate.
2 Wi-Fi doesn't work here.
3 It was a telemarketing call.
4 I'll text you.
5 He keeps ignoring my texts.
6 I'll get back to you later.
7 My battery is running low.
8 I called you earlier but you didn't answer.

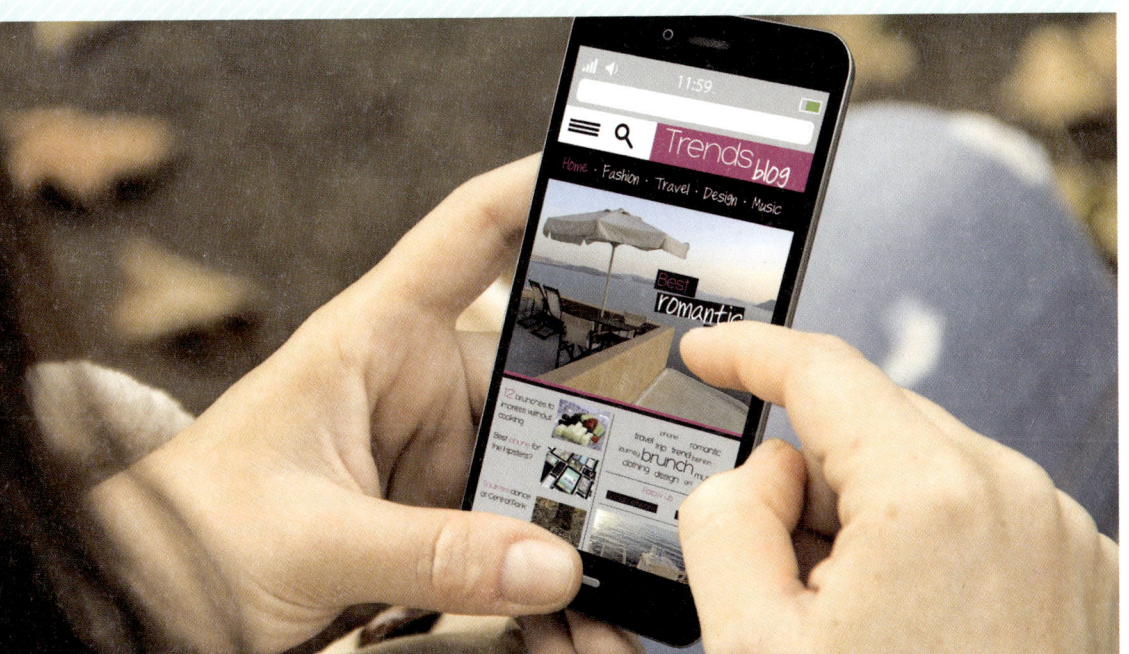

Dialogue Expressions

Complete each dialogue.

1   영화 시작하는데, 전화기 껐어요?
The movie is about to start. Did you turn off your phone?

진동모드로 해놨어요.

2   여기 와이파이가 안 돼요

비밀번호 걸려 있어서 그래요. 카운터에서 물어보세요.
That's because it's password protected. Ask about it at the counter.

3   무슨 전화예요?
Who was that on the phone?

광고 전화예요. 자꾸 새 폰을 사래요.
They keep telling me to buy a new phone.

4   어떤 이유인지 (통화)감이 안 좋아요. 자꾸 끊겨요.
I'm losing you for some reason. The signal keeps breaking off.

문자로 보내줄게요.

1 I put it on vibrate.
2 Wi-Fi doesn't work here.
3 It was a telemarketing call.
4 I'll text you instead.

5 　그 사람이 계속 내 문자를 씹어요.

　둘이 싸웠어요?
　Did you two get into a fight?

6 　지금 통화 가능하세요?
　Are you free to talk right now?

　이따 전화할게요. 윗사람이 불러서요.
　My boss is calling me.

7 　배터리가 얼마 안 남았어요. 보조 배터리도 없는데.
　And I don't have an extra one.

　편의점에 가면 충전할 수 있어요.
　You can recharge it at a convenience store.

8 　아까 전화했는데 안 받으시던데요.

　미안해요. 회의 중이라 못 받았어요.
　Sorry, I couldn't take the call as I was in a meeting.

Answers

5　He keeps ignoring my texts.
6　I'll get back to you later.
7　My battery is running low.
8　I called you earlier but you didn't answer.

DIALOGUE PATTERNS

Complete each sentence.

A 무슨 일로 전화하셨죠?
What is your call regarding?

 면접 때문에 전화드렸습니다.
I'm calling about the job interview.

1 신문 광고 보고 전화드렸습니다.
   I'm calling about

2 내일 회의 때문에 전화드렸습니다.
   I'm calling about

3 선적 건으로 전화드렸습니다.
   I'm calling about

B 계속 잡음이 들리는데요.
I keep getting static.

 전화기 자체에 문제가 있는지 확인해볼게요.
I'll see if there's anything wrong with the phone itself.

4 존이 왔는지 볼게요.
   I'll see if

5 자리에 계신지 볼게요.
   I'll see if

6 그 분이 통화 중이신지 볼게요.
   I'll see if

1 your ad in the newspaper.
2 tomorrow's meeting.
3 a shipment.
4 John is here yet.
5 she is in.
6 he's on the phone.

DIALOGUE STRATEGY

 참고로, 최근 제 전화번호가 바뀌었습니다.
Just so you know, I changed my phone number recently.

 어쩐지, 전화했는데 없는 번호로 나오더라구요.
No wonder it said the number didn't exist when I called you.

Just so you know 참고로

"Just so you know" is a phrase that is usually used when you want to relay useful but not always important information. It is usually put in the beginning of a sentence. A longer, less used version is "I just want to let you know that."

*relay 전달하다

'Just so you know'는 쓸모 있으나 반드시 중요하진 않을 수도 있는 정보에 대해 말할 때 보통 쓰는 표현으로 대개 문장 앞부분에 씁니다. 길이가 약간 더 길고 이보다는 덜 자주 쓰이긴 하지만 'I just want to let you know that'이란 표현도 쓸 수 있습니다.

UNIT 04 Smartphone

Dialogue Listening

A Listen to the dialogue and complete the sentence.

1 The woman asked the man to send her _____

B Listen again and fill in "T" for true or "F" for false.

2 The man got off an elevator. ( )

3 The woman ended up texting the man. ( )

1 the file of a sales report.
여자는 남자에게 판매 보고서 파일을 보내달라고 요청했다.
2 (T) 남자는 엘리베이터에서 내렸다.
3 (F) 여자는 결국 남자에게 문자를 보냈다.

Story Listening

A Listen to the article and complete the sentence.

1 This story is about the world's first

B Listen again and fill in "T" for true or "F" for false.

2 Two companies collaborated to make the world's first cell phone. (　)

3 Martin Cooper was the first to make a telephone. (　)

C Discuss the article by answering the questions below.

4 If you had been in Cooper's shoes, who would you have called and why?

5 Could you live without a cell phone? Why?

1 cell phone call.
   이 이야기는 세계 최초의 휴대전화 통화에 관한 것이다.
2 (F) 두 회사가 세계 최초 휴대폰을 만들기 위해 협력했다.
3 (F) Martin Cooper는 최초로 전화기를 만든 사람이다.
4 자신이 Cooper였다면 누구에게 전화를 걸었을까? 그 이유는?
5 휴대 전화 없이 살 수 있는가? 왜 그러한가?

Script for Dialogue Listening

Amy	Hello? I can't hear you. You keep breaking up.
Paul	Sorry, I'm in the elevator right now.
Amy	Should I just text you?
Paul	Say what? Hold on. I'm getting off.
Amy	Can you hear me now?
Paul	That's much better.
Amy	Can you send me a file of the sales report?
Paul	Wi-Fi doesn't seem to work here. I think it's password protected.
Amy	Well, it's kind of urgent.
Paul	I'll think of a way and call you back.

text 문자를 보내다   get off 내리다   urgent 긴급한

에이미	여보세요? 잘 안 들려요. 계속 끊겨요.
폴	미안해요. 지금 엘리베이터 안이에요.
에이미	문자로 할까요?
폴	뭐라고요? 잠깐만요. 내려요.
에이미	이제 들려요?
폴	훨씬 낫네요.
에이미	판매 보고서 파일 좀 보내줄 수 있어요?
폴	여기 와이파이가 안 되는 것 같아요. 비밀번호가 걸려있는 것 같은데.
에이미	좀 급해요.
폴	방법을 생각해보고 다시 전화 줄게요.

SCRIPT FOR STORY LISTENING

The Story of the First Cell Phone Call

Have you ever wondered who made the first cell phone call and what it was about? On April 3, 1973 an engineer named Martin Cooper made a phone call walking down the street. It was a strange sight and a tremendous achievement at the time. Cooper was the head of a team of engineers at Motorola responsible for the world's first cellular phone.

So who did he call? His mom? His girlfriend? His engineering team? Cooper's first thought was to call his competitor at AT&T, part of a team also working to build a cellular phone. He told his rival, Joel Engel, that he had succeeded and was calling him from the first portable phone. Engel's response? Silence.

tremendous 거대한   achievement 업적   competitor 경쟁자

최초의 휴대 전화 통화 이야기

처음에 누가 휴대 전화로 전화를 걸었고 내용이 무엇이었는지 궁금한 적이 있었는가? 1973년 4월 3일, Martin Cooper라는 기술자가 길을 걸으며 전화를 걸었다. 그때는 이것이 희한한 광경이었고, 엄청난 업적이었다. Cooper는 세계 최초 휴대전화 개발을 담당하고 있던 Motorola사의 기술 책임자였다.

그는 누구에게 전화를 했을까? 엄마? 여자친구? 기술팀? Cooper가 처음으로 전화를 건 대상은 AT&T사의 경쟁자였다. 그도 또한 AT&T사의 기술팀에서 휴대폰을 개발하려고 노력 중이었다. 그는 라이벌인 Joel Engel에게 그가 최초로 휴대폰 개발에 성공하여 전화를 거는 것이라고 말했다. Engel의 응답은 어땠을까? 침묵이었다.

Culture Tip

Skype is a popular telecommunication application with which you can send instant messages, exchange files, and hold conference calls. It is especially popular in America for its video chat function which users can use for free. What chat program is popular in Korea?

*application 응용 프로그램

Skype는 인스턴트 메시지를 보내거나, 파일을 주고 받고, 전화 회의도 가능한 대중적인 통신 프로그램입니다. 특히 사용자들이 무료로 사용할 수 있는 채팅 기능으로 인해 미국에서 인기가 많습니다. 한국에는 어떤 채팅 프로그램이 인기가 있나요?

Idiom Origin

Ring a bell 들어본 적이 있다, 기억나다

If something "rings a bell", it means that it is either familiar to you or causes you to remember something else. Since long ago, bells have been used to remind people of everything from church events to time itself, hence, the term "ring a bell."

무언가가 'ring a bell'한다는 것은 그게 잘 아는 것이거나 뭔가 다른 것을 기억나게 해준다는 말입니다. 오래 전부터 종은 사람들에게 교회 행사부터 시간까지 모든 것을 상기시키는 용도로 이용되어 왔습니다. 그래서 'ring a bell'이란 표현이 생기게 된 것이죠.

 이 번호 들어본 적 있어요? 이 번호로 자꾸 이상한 문자가 와요.
   Does this number **ring a bell?** I've been getting weird SMS's from it.

 그냥 번호를 차단해버려요.
   Just block the number.

Emotions

1 그녀가 날 못살게 해요.
2 제니는 자꾸 이래라 저래라 해요.
3 로이가 뒤에서 날 험담했어요.
4 그냥 요즘 마음이 복잡해요.
5 모두들 기겁을 했어요.
6 요즘은 되는 일이 하나도 없어요.
7 너무 재미있어서 시간 가는 줄 몰랐어요.
8 그 얘기 듣고 온몸에 소름이 돋았어요.

1 She's giving me a hard time.
2 Jenny always bosses me around.
3 Roy talked behind my back.
4 I just have a lot on my mind lately.
5 Everybody totally freaked out.
6 Nothing is going right these days.
7 I was having so much fun I lost track of the time.
8 I got goosebumps all over to hear that.

Dialogue Expressions

Complete each dialogue.

1. 토드가 왜 자꾸 필립을 못살게 구는지 모르겠어요.
   I'm not sure why Todd keeps giving Phillip a hard time.

   그럴 만한 이유가 있겠죠.
   He must have a good reason.

2. 제니는 나한테 자꾸 이래라 저래라 해요.
   Jenny always bosses me around.

   그래요? 나한테는 정말 잘해주는데.
   Really? She is very nice to me.

3. 로이가 뒤에서 날 험담했어요.
   Roy talked behind my back.

   호랑이도 제 말하면 온다더니 저기 오네요.
   Speak of the devil, here he comes.

4. 그 일이 아직 마음에 걸려서 그래요? 잊어버려요.
   Is that still on your mind? Just let it go.

   그냥 요즘 마음이 복잡해요.
   I just have a lot on my mind lately.

1. keeps giving Phillip a hard time.
2. Jenny always bosses me around.
3. Roy talked behind my back.
4. I just have a lot on my mind lately.

5 바퀴벌레가 나와서 모두들 정말 기겁을 했다니까요.

when a cockroach came out.

바퀴벌레 너무 싫어요. 너무 징그럽게 생기지 않았어요?

I hate roaches. Aren't they gross?

6 요즘은 되는 일이 하나도 없어요.

힘내요. 곧 나아질 거예요.

Cheer up. I'm sure things will look up soon.

7 늦겠어요. 벌써 8시예요.

We are going to be late. It's already eight o'clock.

벌써요? 너무 재미있어서 시간 가는 줄 몰랐어요.

Already?

8 시내에서 연쇄살인사건이 났어요.

There have been a number of serial killings in town.

 그 얘기 듣고 온몸에 소름이 돋았어요.

5 Everybody totally freaked out
6 Nothing is going right these days.
7 I was having so much fun I lost track of the time.
8 I got goosebumps all over to hear that.

DIALOGUE PATTERNS

Complete each sentence.

A

 그 사람이 나를 대하는 방식이 맘에 안 들어요.
I don't like the way he treats me.

 그 사람 원래 그래요. 마음 쓰지 마요.
That's just the way he is. Don't let it bother you.

1 그 사람 말투가 맘에 안 들어요.
I don't like the way

2 그 사람 옷 입는 게 맘에 안 들어요.
I don't like the way

3 그 사람 있는 그대로가 좋아요.
I like him the way

B

 진짜 억울했겠어요.
You must have been pretty resentful.

 그랬죠. 말 그대로, 걔가 내 뒤통수를 친 거죠.
I was. He stabbed me in the back.

4 막막했겠어요.
You must have been

5 맘 상했겠어요.
You must have been

6 제법 무서웠겠어요.
You must have been

1 he talks to me.
2 he dresses.
3 he is.
4 at a loss.
5 upset.
6 pretty scared.

DIALOGUE STRATEGY

 사라가 그 문제를 가지고 너무 예민하게 구는 것 같아요.
I feel that Sarah is being too sensitive on the issue.

 반대로, 저는 그녀가 걱정할 만한 것 같은데요.
On the contrary, I think she has every right to be concerned.

On the contrary 그와 반대로

When you have an opinion that is contrary to someone else's, you can start by stating "On the contrary." The phrase is often used when your statement is the total opposite of the previous statement. It is stronger in context than "Actually" which can be used in similar situations.

*opposite 반대되는

상대의 의견과 상반되는 의견이 있을 경우, 'On the contrary'로 말을 시작할 수 있습니다. 이 표현은 자신의 말이 이전의 내용과 완전히 반대될 때 자주 쓰이는데 비슷한 상황에서 쓸 수 있는 'Actually'보다 문맥상 강한 느낌을 줍니다.

DIALOGUE LISTENING

A Listen to the dialogue and complete the sentence.

1 The man was upset because his wife _____

B Listen again and fill in "T" for true or "F" for false.

2 The woman has a pleasant relationship with her clients. (   )

3 The man suggested that the woman be firm. (   )

1 nagged at him.
    남자는 아내의 잔소리 때문에 언짢아했다.
2 (F) 여자는 고객들과 원만한 관계를 유지하고 있다.
3 (T) 남자는 여자가 단호하게 대처할 것을 제안했다.

Story Listening

A   Listen to the article and complete the sentence.

1   Happy people have more _____ goals than unhappy people.

B   Listen again and fill in "T" for true or "F" for false.

2   Happy and unhappy people have similar goals. (　)

3   Unhappy people often set unreachable goals. (　)

C   Discuss the article by answering the questions below.

4   Are you happy? Why or why not?

5   What are your goals in life? Do you think they are attainable?

1   modest
행복한 사람들은 불행한 사람들에 비해 좀더 평범한 목표를 세운다.
2   (F) 행복한 사람과 그렇지 않은 사람은 비슷한 목표를 가지고 있다.
3   (T) 불행한 사람들은 종종 이루기 힘든 목표를 설정한다.
4   자신은 행복한가? 왜 그런가? 혹은 왜 그렇지 않은가?
5   자신의 인생의 목표는 무엇인가? 그 목표가 실현 가능하다고 보는가?

● Script for Dialogue Listening

Alice	Is there something wrong? You look really down.
Jim	My wife nagged at me for being late last night.
Alice	Why were you late?
Jim	I just had a couple of drinks with friends. I wasn't even that late but she got sore and won't even talk to me.
Alice	It must have been tough.
Jim	I'll be okay. By the way, how are things going with your clients?
Alice	They still push me around. It's suffocating.
Jim	Don't let it bother you.
Alice	I just wish they would see the issue from my side.
Jim	Be more firm with them and I'm sure they'll come around.

nag at ~에게 잔소리하다   suffocate 질식시키다   bother 괴롭히다   be firm with 단호하다   come around 정신 차리다

앨리스	무슨 걱정 있어요? 얼굴이 어두워 보이는데.
짐	어젯밤 늦게 들어왔다고 아내가 잔소리를 하잖아요.
앨리스	왜 늦었는데요?
짐	친구들하고 몇 잔 했죠. 그렇게 늦지도 않았는데 삐져서 말도 안 해요.
앨리스	괴로웠겠네요.
짐	괜찮을 거예요. 그나저나 고객들하고는 어때요?
앨리스	갑질은 여전하죠. 정말 숨막혀요.
짐	마음 쓰지 말아요.
앨리스	입장을 바꿔놓고 생각하면 좋겠어요.
짐	단호하게 해보세요. 그러면 정신 차릴 거예요.

● SCRIPT FOR STORY LISTENING

The Secret to Happiness

What are the differences between happy and unhappy people? For one thing, happy people are known to value things they already have. They also have modest, reachable goals. In other words, they are happy with what they have. On the other hand, unhappy people often have lofty and unrealistic goals. Their desires prevent them from appreciating what they have. Never able to live up to their ambitions, they are unsatisfied and thus never happy.

In many cases, the goals people set for themselves are related to how they feel. People who set and reach higher goals are no happier than people who set and reach modest goals. The more attainable and modest their goals, the more likely people are to feel good about themselves.

value 가치있게 여기다   reachable 달성 가능한   lofty 아주 높은   appreciate 감사히 여기다
ambition 욕망   modest 보통의   attainable 달성 가능한

행복의 비밀

행복한 사람과 불행한 사람의 차이점은 무엇일까? 그 중 한 가지로, 행복한 사람은 그들이 이미 가지고 있는 것을 소중히 여긴다고 알려져 있다. 그들은 또한 어렵지 않고, 달성 가능한 목표를 가지고 있다. 즉, 그들은 그들이 현재 가지고 있는 것에 행복하다. 반대로, 불행한 사람들은 종종 아주 크고 실현 가능성이 낮은 목표를 가지고 있다. 욕심으로 인하여 그들은 현재 가진 것에 대해 감사하지 않는다. 그들의 야망에 결코 부응할 수 없기에, 그들은 만족하지 못하고, 결코 행복하지 못하다.

많은 경우, 사람들 스스로 정하는 목표들은 그들이 어떻게 느끼는지와 관련이 있다. 더 높은 목표를 정해서 그것을 달성하는 사람들은 보통의 목표를 설정하고 달성하는 사람보다 더 행복하지 않다. 그들의 목표가 더 달성 가능하고 평범할수록 사람들은 자신에 대해 더 만족하는 경향이 있다.

Culture Tip

In America, if someone bumps into you, you're likely to hear "excuse me" or "pardon me." People also make apologies for the simplest things like coughing and burping. If you sneeze, you're even likely to hear "bless you." Do people usually apologize in Korea in these situations?

*bump into ~에 부딪치다 burp 트림하다

미국에서는 누구와 부딪치면 보통 'excuse me'나 'pardon me'라는 말을 듣게 됩니다. 기침이나 트림 같은 사소한 것에도 사과를 하고 상대가 재채기를 할 경우엔 'bless you'라고 말해주기까지 합니다. 한국에서도 이럴 때 보통 사과를 하나요?

Idiom Origin

Have butterflies in one's stomach   가슴이 조마조마하고 긴장되다

This term has been used to describe the sick, unpleasant feeling people get when they are nervous. The feeling has often been described as "tickling" due to a reduction of blood flow to the stomach. This mild feeling was said to bring up images of butterflies due to their delicate and tickling perception.

*tickling 간지럼 perception 지각

이 표현은 사람들이 긴장할 때 느끼는 메스껍고 불편한 느낌을 표현할 때 사용되어 왔습니다. 이 느낌은 위장으로 가는 혈류 감소로 인해 '간질간질하다'고 표현되어져 왔는데 이 가벼운 느낌이 미세하고 간지럽게 느껴져서 나비의 이미지를 떠올리게 되었다고 합니다.

 이제 'K팝스타' 최종 우승자를 발표하나 봐요.
They are going to announce the final winner of *K-pop Star*.

 내가 다 가슴이 조마조마하네.
I have butterflies in my stomach.

Unit 06 Holiday

1 겨우 입석표를 구했어요.
2 차례는 어디서 지내요?
3 음력설에 왜 떡국을 먹는 거예요?
4 세배 이렇게 하는 거 맞아요?
5 세뱃돈 받는 게 제일 좋죠.
6 이번 추석은 일요일이에요.
7 벌초한 후엔 절을 해요.
8 왜 추석에 반달 모양 송편을 먹을까요?

1 I barely got ahold of standing room tickets.
2 Where do you hold memorial services for your ancestors?
3 Why do we eat rice cake soup on Lunar New Year's Day?
4 Is this how you do the New Year's bow?
5 Getting New Year's gift money is the best part.
6 Chuseok falls on a Sunday this year.
7 We bow after cutting the weeds around the graves.
8 Why do we eat half moon-shaped songpyeons on Chuseok?

DIALOGUE EXPRESSIONS

Complete each dialogue.

1   이번 설에 고향 가세요?
    Are you visiting your hometown this New Year?

    네. 겨우 입석표를 구했어요.
    Yes, but

2   차례는 어디서 지내요?

    우리집은 큰집에서 지내요.
    My family holds them at my oldest uncle's house.

3   설날에 왜 떡국을 먹는 거예요?

    떡국을 먹어야 한 살을 먹는대요.
    We need to eat rice cake soup to be a year older.

4   세배 이렇게 하는 거 맞아요?

    네. 그런데 무릎을 꿇은 후에 머리를 숙여야 해요.
    Yes, but you have to lower your head after kneeling.

Answers

1 I barely got ahold of standing room tickets.
2 Where do you hold memorial services for your ancestors?
3 Why do we eat rice cake soup on Lunar New Year's Day?
4 Is this how you do the New Year's bow?

5　　설날에 가장 좋았던 게 뭐였어요?
　　　What was the best part of Lunar New Year's Day?

　　　어른들한테 절하고 세뱃돈 받는 거였죠.
　　　　　　　　　　　　　　　　　　after bowing down to the adults.

6　　이번 추석은 일요일이에요.

　　　많은 날 중에 왜 하필 일요일이지?
　　　Why Sunday of all days?

7　　성묘 가서 뭐 해요?
　　　What do you do when you go to the gravesite?

　　　벌초한 다음에 음식 차려놓고 절 해요.
　　　We set up a table and bow,

8　　왜 추석에 반달 모양 송편을 먹는 거예요?

　　　반달이 계속 커져 보름달이 되듯 일이 잘 되라구요.
　　　We eat them to be successful as half moons grow to be full moons.

Answers

5　It was getting New Year's gift money
6　Chuseok falls on a Sunday this year.
7　after cutting the weeds around the graves.
8　Why do we eat half moon-shaped songpyeons on Chuseok?

DIALOGUE PATTERNS

Complete each sentence.

  운전을 오래 했더니만 전신이 다 쑤셔요.
I'm aching all over after driving for so long.

저는 제사 음식 장만**하느라 힘들었어요.**
I had a hard time preparing all the food for the ritual.

1 손님 치르느라 힘들었어요.
   I had a hard time

2 전 부치느라 힘들었어요.
   I had a hard time

3 잔소리 듣느라 힘들었어요.
   I had a hard time

  명절에 남편이 일 좀 도와주나요?
Does your husband help you out during the holidays?

아니요. **맨날** 손도 까딱 않고 누워서 TV만 보고 **있죠.**
No. **He is always** lying down and watching TV without lifting a hand.

4 맨날 음식 타박해요.
   He is always

5 맨날 별거 아닌 거 갖고 징징대요.
   He is always

6 맨날 남의 일에 간섭해요.
   He is always

1 hosting all the guests.
2 griddling the pancakes.
3 being scolded.
4 grumbling about food.
5 whining about trivial things.
6 nosing into other's business.

Dialogue Strategy

 추석 얘기가 나와서 말인데, 날짜가 언제예요?
Speaking of Chuseok, when is it?

 음력으로 8월 15일이니까 양력 9월 27일이에요.
It's August 15 on the lunar calendar and September 27 on the solar calendar.

Speaking of ~얘기가 나와서 말인데, 말 나온 김에

"Speaking of" is used when a certain topic has come up and you want to talk about it. It's a good phrase to use when you want to change the topic. A similar expression is "While we're on the subject" which is also usually used at the beginning of a sentence.

'Speaking of'는 특정 화제가 언급되어 그것에 대해 말하고자 할 때 쓰는데 주제를 전환시킬 때 요긴하게 쓸 수 있는 표현입니다. 유사 표현으로는 'While we're on the subject'가 있고 마찬가지로 문장 앞에 옵니다.

Dialogue Listening

A Listen to the dialogue and complete the sentence.

1 The man is planning to visit his family on

B Listen again and fill in "T" for true or "F" for false.

2 There's a chance the man is going to take the bus. (   )

3 The woman suggests that the man's family play Go-Stop. (   )

1 New Year's Day.
   남자는 설날에 집에 갈 계획이다.
2 (T) 남자는 버스를 타고 갈 수도 있다.
3 (F) 여자는 남자 가족에게 고스톱을 치라고 제안한다.

Story Listening

A Listen to the article and complete the sentence.

1 On Nyepi, people pretend that the island is _____ to fool the devils.

B Listen again and fill in "T" for true or "F" for false.

2 Parades and feasts are held on the actual day of Nyepi. ( )

3 People remain silent for all six days of Nyepi. ( )

C Discuss the article by answering the questions below.

4 What similarities and differences do Nyepi and the Korean New Year have?

5 How would you explain Korea's New Year holiday to foreigners?

1 empty
   Nyepi 당일날, 사람들은 악귀들을 속이기 위해 섬에 아무도 없는 척한다.
2 (F) 행렬과 축제는 Nyepi 당일에 열린다.
3 (F) Nyepi 연휴 6일 동안 사람들은 말을 하지 않는다.
4 Nyepi와 한국의 설날이 비슷한 점과 다른 점은 무엇인가?
5 한국의 설날을 외국인에게 어떻게 설명할 것인가?

● SCRIPT FOR DIALOGUE LISTENING

Mindy	Are you going to visit your family this New Year's Day?
Ken	Yes, but I haven't gotten train tickets yet.
Mindy	Really? You better hurry. Even standing room tickets might be sold out.
Ken	I'm actually thinking about taking the express bus this time.
Mindy	Won't it take a long time to get there?
Ken	I'm in no hurry to get there. My family always fights when they get together.
Mindy	Maybe you can be a peacemaker?
Ken	Oh, no. I don't want to get involved. It's always something trivial.
Mindy	Or maybe you can suggest playing yut?
Ken	I'm not sure if that will work. If we play a game, we always play Go-Stop.

standing room 입석   express bus 고속버스   peacemaker 중재자   get involved 관여하다   trivial 사소한

민디	이번 설에 집에 가세요?
켄	네, 그런데 기차표를 못 끊었어요.
민디	정말요? 서두르세요. 입석표도 매진됐을 수 있어요.
켄	이번엔 고속버스 타고 갈까 해요.
민디	가는 데 오래 걸리지 않을까요?
켄	바쁠 거 없거든요. 우리 가족은 모이면 맨날 싸워요.
민디	중재를 하시면 되지 않을까요?
켄	아뇨, 전 끼어들고 싶지 않아요. 항상 사소한 걸로 그래요.
민디	윷놀이 하자고 해보세요.
켄	될지 잘 모르겠어요. 게임하면 맨날 고스톱이나 치거든요.

● SCRIPT FOR STORY LISTENING

Nyepi: The Day of Silence

Imagine living in total silence for an entire day. Believe it or not, people on the island of Bali do this for the Hindu holiday Nyepi to celebrate the new year. The six day long holiday is commemorated with parades and feasts which are held to keep devils away.

However, on the actual day of Nyepi, people stay at home and spend the day in total silence. This is to deceive the devils into believing that the island is empty. No sounds are allowed; television, radio and even conversations are prohibited. Roads are off limits to cars. Shops and restaurants are closed. Even tourists aren't allowed to go outside their hotels. It is said that should an airplane fly over Bali, the island would appear to be uninhabited.

commemorate 기념하다 feast 축제 prohibited 금지된 off limits 접근 금지
uninhabited 아무도 살지 않는

Nyepi: 침묵의 날

하루 종일 완전한 침묵 속에서 사는 것을 상상해 보라. 믿거나 말거나, 발리인들은 힌두교 공휴일인 Nyepi에 새해를 기념하기 위해서 이렇게 한다. 6일 간의 긴 공휴일 동안 악귀들을 쫓기 위해 벌이는 축제와 행렬로 기념한다.

그런데 정작 Nyepi 당일 날에는 사람들이 집에 머무르면서 완전한 침묵 속에 보낸다. 이것은 발리에 아무도 살지 않는 척 악귀를 속이기 위한 것이다. 어떠한 소음도 허락되지 않는다. TV, 라디오, 심지어 대화도 금지된다. 도로는 차들이 다닐 수 없다. 상점과 식당들은 문을 닫는다. 심지어 여행객들조차 호텔 밖으로 나갈 수 없다. 발리 위로 비행기가 지나가면, 이 섬은 무인도처럼 보일 것이라고 한다.

While there aren't exact equivalents to Lunar New Year's Day and Chuseok in America, there are days when similar things are celebrated. On holidays like Thanksgiving and Christmas, families gather and have traditional meals. One of the more popular dishes is roast turkey, which is served on Thanksgiving. What special dishes are served in Korea?

미국에서 음력설과 추석과 똑같은 날은 없지만 비슷한 날은 추수감사절과 크리스마스입니다. 이날엔 한국처럼 가족들이 모여서 전통음식을 먹습니다. 더 대중적인 음식 중 하나는 추수감사절에 먹는 구운 칠면조입니다. 한국에는 어떤 특별한 음식이 나오나요?

Beat around the bush 돌려 말하다, 뜸들이다

"Beat around the bush" means to speak vaguely, or to delay to waste time. This saying originated from bird hunting. Hunters beat bushes in order to rouse bird flocks before shooting at them. This indirect way of hunting gave the impression of wasting time, hence the term.

*rouse 자극하다 flock 무리

'Beat around the bush'란 모호하게 말하거나 지체시켜 시간을 낭비하는 것을 뜻합니다. 이 표현은 새 사냥에서 유래하였는데 사냥꾼들은 새에게 총을 쏘기 전에 새떼들을 자극하려고 덤불 주위를 두드렸습니다. 이런 간접적인 사냥 방식이 시간을 낭비한다는 인상을 주었고 그래서 이런 표현이 생기게 된 것입니다.

 하루 종일 설거지했더니 팔도 아프고 허리도 아프고…
My arms and back hurt after washing dishes all day…

 빙빙 돌리지 말고 결론을 말해요.
Don't beat around the bush and get to the point.

Unit 07 Dress Code

1 회사 갈 땐 주로 정장을 입어요.
2 그 사람은 옷을 잘 입어요.
3 보통 그렇게 머리를 뒤로 묶어요?
4 자켓 단추를 채워요.
5 향수 좀 뿌렸어요.
6 반드시 굽이 낮은 신발을 신으세요.
7 쫙 빼 입으셨네요.
8 긴 면바지를 입으세요.

1 I usually wear suits to work.
2 He is a sharp dresser.
3 Do you usually tie your hair back like that?
4 Button your jacket.
5 I'm wearing a perfume.
6 Make sure to wear low-heeled shoes.
7 You're all dressed up.
8 You should wear long khaki pants.

Dialogue Expressions

Complete each dialogue.

1   전 회사원이라 회사갈 때 주로 정장을 입어요.
    As an office worker,

    그래도 금요일엔 편한 옷으로 입지 않나요?
    Don't you dress more casually on Fridays, though?

2   새로 뽑은 사람 어떤 것 같아요?
    What do you think about the new recruit?

    아직 잘 모르지만 옷은 확실히 잘 입네요.
    I'm not sure yet, but

3   보통 그렇게 머리를 뒤로 묶어요?

    아뇨. 오늘은 머리가 엉망이라 묶은 거예요.
    No. I tied it up today because it was a mess.

4   아주 좋은 냄새가 나요. 뭐 뿌렸어요?
    You smell really great. Are you wearing something?

    네. 향수 뿌렸는데, 냄새 좋죠?
    Yes,   Smells good, doesn't it?

1 I usually wear suits to work.
2 he sure is a sharp dresser.
3 Do you usually tie your hair back like that?
4 I'm wearing a perfume.

5   회의 전에 자켓 단추 꼭 채우세요.

     왜요? 단추를 안 잠그면 예의에 어긋나나요?
     Why? Is it improper to leave it unbuttoned?

6   세미나 드레스 코드로 알아둬야 할 게 있어요?
     Anything I should know about the dress code to the seminar?

     네. 반드시 굽이 낮은 신발을 신으세요.
     Yes.

7   쫙 빼 입으셨네요. 뭔 일 있어요?
     What's the occasion?

     오후에 결혼식 가야 해서요.
     I have to go to a wedding in the afternoon.

8   드레스 코드가 스마트 캐주얼이면 뭘 입는 거예요?
     If the dress code is smart casual, what should I wear?

     긴 면바지에 셔츠면 되고 넥타이는 안 해도 돼요.
     but no tie.

*khaki pants 면바지

5   Make sure to button your jacket before the meeting.
6   Make sure to wear low-heeled shoes.
7   You're all dressed up.
8   You should wear long khaki pants and a shirt,

Dialogue Patterns

Complete each sentence.

A 화장을 진하게 하면 안 돼요.
You're not allowed to put on heavy makeup.

 립스틱만 조금 바른 거예요.
I only put on some lipstick.

1 민소매 입으면 안 돼요.
   You're not allowed to

2 진한 향수를 뿌리면 안 돼요.
   You're not allowed to

3 문신을 하면 안 돼요.
   You're not allowed to

B 머리를 세워볼까 생각 중이에요.
I'm thinking of spiking my hair.

 정말로요? 윗사람이 안 좋아할 텐데요.
You're sure? I don't think the boss will like that.

4 젤을 바를까 생각 중이에요.
   I'm thinking of

5 명품지갑 하나 살까 생각 중이에요.
   I'm thinking of

6 땡땡이 무늬 넥타이를 맬까 생각 중이에요.
   I'm thinking of

Answers

1 wear sleeveless shirts.
2 wear strong perfume.
3 get tattoos.
4 applying some gel.
5 buying a brand-name purse.
6 wearing a polka-dot tie.

DIALOGUE STRATEGY

 정말 이 꽃무늬로 가야 된다고 생각해요?
You really think I should go with this floral one?

다시 생각해보니까 무늬 없는 게 더 적합하겠어요.
On second thought, I think the plain one is more suitable.

On second thought 다시 생각해보니까

"On second thought" is used when one has a change of mind. After stating an opinion, you can make a contrary or different opinion by starting the new sentence with "On second thought." It suggests that you had a change of mind after thinking about it for a second time.

'On second thought'는 마음이 바뀌었을 때 씁니다. 어떤 의견을 제시한 다음에 'On second thought'로 새로운 문장을 시작하면서 앞서 말한 것과 반대되거나 다른 의견을 제시할 수 있습니다. 이 표현은 재차 생각해보고는 마음이 바뀌었음을 표시하는 것입니다.

Dialogue Listening

A Listen to the dialogue and complete the sentence.

1 The man is telling the woman about _____.

B Listen again and fill in "T" for true or "F" for false.

2 The man suggests that employees bring both casual and formal clothes. (   )

3 The man says that they will be hiking at the workshop. (   )

1 the dress code for a workshop.
남자는 여자에게 워크샵 복장 규정에 대해 말하고 있다.
2 (T) 남자는 직원들이 편한 옷과 정장을 모두 가져와야 한다고 한다.
3 (F) 남자는 워크샵에서 등산을 할 거라고 말한다.

Story Listening

A Listen to the article and complete the sentence.

1 The Swiss bank UBS has a very _____ dress code.

B Listen again and fill in "T" for true or "F" for false.

2 Women at UBS were required to use a specific type of perfume. ( )

3 Men at UBS were required to wear bow ties to work. ( )

C Discuss the article by answering the questions below.

4 Do you think UBS's dress code went too far?

5 What is your company's dress code?

1 detailed
   스위스 은행 UBS에는 굉장히 세부적인 복장 규정이 있다.
2 (T) UBS에서 근무하는 여성들은 특정 향수를 사용하도록 되어 있었다.
3 (F) UBS에서 근무하는 남성들은 회사에 올 때 나비넥타이를 매야 했다.
4 UBS 복장 규정이 지나쳤다고 생각하는가?
5 자신이 다니는 회사의 복장 규정에는 어떤 것이 있는가?

● Script for Dialogue Listening

Max	Everyone, I have an announcement. We are having our annual workshop next Friday.
Tina	What's the dress code for the workshop?
Max	Casual wear is acceptable in the morning, but we have to dress up for dinner.
Tina	So, do we have to bring a suit, tie, dress shoes, and a dress shirt?
Max	No, not that formal. A polo or dress shirt, khaki pants, and a blazer will be fine.
Tina	Are we going to play any sports?
Max	We are going to play basketball, so bring your sneakers.
Tina	Anything else?
Max	It might be sunny. So I also recommend that you bring hats and shades.
Tina	Great. I'll tell everyone in my department.

announcement 발표   acceptable 허용되는   dress up 차려입다   dress shirt 와이셔츠
formal 격식을 차린   khaki pants 면바지   blazer 콤보 상의   sneakers 운동화   shades 선글라스

맥스	여러분, 발표할 게 있습니다. 다음 주 금요일에 연례 워크샵이 있을 겁니다.
티나	워크숍의 복장 규정은 어떻게 되나요?
맥스	오전에는 캐주얼을 입어도 되지만, 저녁식사 때는 정장을 입어야 합니다.
티나	그럼, 정장, 넥타이, 정장 구두, 그리고 와이셔츠를 가져와야 하나요?
맥스	아니요, 그렇게까지 갖출 필요는 없어요. 편한 반소매 셔츠나 와이셔츠, 면바지, 그리고 블레이저면 됩니다.
티나	운동도 해요?
맥스	농구를 할 거예요. 그러니 운동화를 가져 오세요.
티나	또 다른 거 필요한 게 있어요?
맥스	햇빛이 강할 수 있으니 모자와 선글라스도 가져오면 좋을 거예요.
티나	알겠습니다. 부서 사람들에게 알릴게요.

● SCRIPT FOR STORY LISTENING

The 44-page Dress Code

   Does your company have a dress code? Dress codes can vary from casual to strict depending on the company. However, Swiss bank, UBS, has been criticized for its extremely detailed 44-page dress code.

   The dress code said that men had to wear ties that matched the "bone structure of their face." Women had to wear skin-colored underwear, and were told how to apply make-up, and what kind of perfume to wear. Acceptable colors for stockings and nail polish were also listed. Moreover, all employees had to wear wristwatches to signal "trustworthiness and a serious concern for punctuality." UBS is famous for its painstaking attention to detail. This has been credited as the secret of its success, but its dress code apparently took things too far.

vary 가지각색이다   extremely 지극히   bone structure 골격   acceptable 허용되는
nail polish 매니큐어   wristwatch 손목시계   trustworthiness 신뢰성   punctuality 시간 엄수
painstaking 공들인   apparently 명백히

44페이지에 달하는 복장 규정

   여러분 회사는 복장 규정을 가지고 있는가? 복장 규정은 회사에 따라 편한 복장부터 정장까지 다양할 수 있다. 그러나 스위스 은행인 UBS가 지나치게 자세히 서술된 44페이지 분량에 달하는 복장 규정으로 비판받고 있다.

   그 복장 규정에는 남자들은 그들의 얼굴 구조와 잘 맞는 넥타이를 매고 여자들은 살색 속옷을 입어야 하고, 화장은 어떻게 해야 하는지 그리고 어떤 종류의 향수를 뿌려야 하는지 지시되어 있다. 착용 가능한 스타킹의 색상과 매니큐어 색상도 명시되어 있다. 게다가 모든 직원들은 신뢰와 철저한 시간 엄수를 의미하기 위해 손목 시계를 차야 했다. UBS는 이런 세부적인 것에 주의를 기울이는 것으로 유명하다. 이것은 성공의 비밀이기도 하겠지만 복장에 관한 규정은 분명히 도를 지나쳤다.

Culture Tip

For formal events in America, the dress code for men is tuxedos or suits with ties. Women usually wear cocktail dresses. For smart, casual wear men put on jackets, dress or khaki slacks, and shirts without ties. Women usually wear cotton dresses, skirts, or pants. What dress codes are there in your country?

*slacks 바지

미국에서 격식을 차린 행사를 할 때 남성의 드레스 코드는 턱시도나 정장에 타이를 매는 것이고 여성은 주로 칵테일 드레스를 착용합니다. 스마트 캐주얼일 경우 남성은 자켓과 정장 바지 또는 면바지에 셔츠를 입는 정도이며 넥타이는 하지 않아도 됩니다. 여성은 보통 편안한 면 드레스, 치마 또는 바지를 입습니다. 여러분의 나라에는 어떤 드레스 코드가 있나요?

Idiom Origin

Keep one's shirt on 진정하다

"Keep one's shirt on" means to stay calm. It is often used to calm down an overly excited person or a person in a rush. The term originated from the fact that people would traditionally take their shirts off before beginning a fistfight.

*fistfight 주먹다짐

'Keep one's shirt on'은 진정하라는 의미로, 과도하게 흥분하거나 서두르는 사람을 진정시킬 때 자주 사용되는 표현입니다. 이 표현은 사람들이 주먹다짐을 하기 전에 통상적으로 셔츠를 벗어 던지는 것에서 유래하였습니다.

 저 여자가 입은 미니스커트와 배꼽티는 이 자리에 정말 부적절해요.
That woman's miniskirt and crop top are really inappropriate here.

 진정해요. 다 제멋에 사는 거 아니겠어요?
Keep your shirt on. There's no accounting for taste.

Unit 08
Meetings

1 회의 의제가 뭐예요?
2 누가 회의록을 작성할 거죠?
3 이 유인물 좀 나눠주세요.
4 시간이 없어요.
5 다수결로 정할게요.
6 저는 찬성이에요.
7 만장일치로 통과됐어요.
8 회의를 마무리하죠

1 What's on the agenda?
2 Who's going to take the minutes for the meeting?
3 Please hand out these sheets.
4 We're running out of time.
5 We'll make the decision by a majority vote.
6 As for me, I'm for it.
7 It was carried by a unanimous vote.
8 Let's wrap up the meeting.

Dialogue Expressions

Complete each dialogue.

1   오늘 회의 의제가 뭐예요?

  실은 오늘 다룰 게 많아요.
  We have lots to cover today actually.

2   모두 와주셔서 감사합니다. 회의를 시작할까요?
  Thank you all for coming. Are we ready to start the meeting?

  누가 회의록을 작성할 거죠?

3   이 유인물을 나눠주세요.

  네. 한 사람당 한 부 맞죠?
  Sure. One sheet per person, right?

4   죄송한데요, 시간이 없어요.
  Excuse me, but

  5분밖에 안 걸릴 거예요.
  This will only take five more minutes.

1 What's on the agenda for today?
2 Who's going to take the minutes for the meeting?
3 Please hand out these sheets.
4 we're running out of time.

5 이 문제에 대해 투표하는 게 어때요?

   Why don't we have a vote on the issue?

   좋은 생각이에요. 다수결로 정할게요.

   That's a good idea.

6 이 제안에 찬성하시나요? 저는 찬성이에요.

   Is everybody in favor of the proposal?

   저는 반대예요.

   I'm against it.

7 투표 결과가 어땠어요?

   What was the result of the vote?

   만장일치로 통과됐어요.

8 다 다룬 것 같네요.

   I think we've covered everything.

   좋아요. 그럼 회의를 마무리하죠

   OK, then

Answers

5 We'll make the decision by a majority vote.
6 As for me, I'm for it.
7 It was carried by a unanimous vote.
8 let's wrap up the meeting.

Dialogue Patterns

Complete each sentence.

A 내일 컨퍼런스 준비 다 됐어요?
Are you ready for the conference tomorrow?

 글쎄요. 여러 사람 앞에서 말하는 게 익숙하지가 않아요.
Not really. **I'm not used to** talking in public.

1 전 화상 회의에 익숙하지 않아요.
I'm not used to

2 그렇게 큰 회의를 주재하는 건 익숙하지 않아요.
I'm not used to

3 파워포인트 같은 툴을 사용하는 게 익숙하지 않아요.
I'm not used to

B 지금 직원 회의 중입니다.
I'm in the middle of a staff meeting.

 네. 다시 전화 드리겠습니다.
OK. I'll call you back.

4 뭣 좀 하는 중이에요.
I'm in the middle of

5 다음 회의 시간과 장소를 잡고 있는 중이에요.
I'm in the middle of

6 우리는 열띤 토론 중이었어요.
We were in the middle of

1 video conferences.
2 chairing such big conferences.
3 using tools like PowerPoint.
4 something.
5 arranging a time and place for the next meeting.
6 a heated argument.

Dialogue Strategy

이건 민주주의적인 방식으로 해야 한다고 봅니다.
I think we should do this in a democratic way.

다른 말로, 투표를 하자는 거군요.
In other words, you want to have a vote.

In other words 다른 말로 하자면

When you want to clarify something that was said, you can use "in other words." It means you're going to rephrase the statement so that it is more clearly understood by you and perhaps other people.

*clarify 명확히 하다   rephrase 바꾸어 말하다

앞에 나온 말의 의미를 분명히 하고자 할 때 'in other words'를 쓸 수 있습니다. 이 말은 본인과 다른 사람들까지 명확히 이해시키기 위해서 그 말을 다시 바꾸어 말하겠다는 의미입니다.

Dialogue Listening

A Listen to the dialogue and complete the sentence.

1 The meeting is about a _____

B Listen again and fill in "T" for true or "F" for false.

2 The CEO is going to preside over the meeting. (   )

3 The woman is going to take the minutes for the meeting. (   )

1 security issue.
회의는 보안에 관련된 것이다.
2 (T) CEO가 회의를 주재할 것이다.
3 (F) 여자는 회의록을 작성할 것이다.

Story Listening

A Listen to the article and complete the sentence.

1 Business meetings may be held in _____ in Asia.

B Listen again and fill in "T" for true or "F" for false.

2 Long business hours encourage people to do business in strange places. ( )

3 In Korea, business meetings always continue in casual locations. ( )

C Discuss the article by answering the questions below.

4 Which do you prefer, a strict business meeting or a casual one?

5 How often do you have meetings? Have you ever fallen asleep in a meeting?

1 unconventional locations
  아시아에서는 때로 독특한 장소에서 업무 회의가 열린다.
2 (T) 긴 업무 시간으로 인해 사람들은 이상한 장소에서 회의를 하게 된다.
3 (F) 한국에서의 업무 회의는 항상 편안한 장소에서 이어진다.
4 격식을 차린 업무 회의를 선호하는가, 아니면 격식을 차리지 않은 회의를 선호하는가?
5 회의를 얼마나 자주 갖는가? 회의에서 잠이 든 적이 있는가?

Script for Dialogue Listening

Bianca　　What's the emergency meeting about?
Jerry　　It's about a security issue.
Bianca　　Did something happen?
Jerry　　Apparently someone hacked into the company's database last night.
Bianca　　That's serious. Is the CEO going to be there?
Jerry　　Yes, Mr. Wallace himself will be presiding.
Bianca　　Should I bring anything?
Jerry　　Just bring the usual office supplies and the minutes from the last security meeting.
Bianca　　How long do you think it will last?
Jerry　　Hopefully it won't take too long.

emergency meeting 긴급 회의　security 보안　apparently 듣자[보아]하니
preside (회의 등을) 주재하다　office supply 사무용품　minutes 회의록

비앙카　　무슨 긴급 회의예요?
제리　　　보안문제 관련한 거예요.
비앙카　　무슨 일 있었어요?
제리　　　듣자 하니 지난 밤에 누군가 회사 데이터베이스를 해킹했대요.
비앙카　　심각하네요. CEO도 참석한대요?
제리　　　네. 미스터 Wallace가 직접 회의 주재한대요.
비앙카　　뭐 가져가야 해요?
제리　　　사무용품하고 지난번 보안회의 회의록만 가져오면 돼요.
비앙카　　얼마나 걸릴까요?
제리　　　너무 오래 걸리지 않길 바래야죠.

● SCRIPT FOR STORY LISTENING

Weird Places for Business Meetings

Executives in Asia have done business at places such as roller coasters, baseball stadiums, and even prisons. One Hong Kong executive says that there's a social aspect to doing business in Asia. Moreover due to long working hours, business meetings are sometimes arranged at strange, but convenient places like bars, clubs, and hot springs. Casual conversation in these places may turn into impromptu business meetings.

Even in Korea, formal meetings sometimes move from the formal office environment to more casual locations to encourage informal discussion. Casual locations could be as conventional as coffee shops or as cultural as karaoke bars and saunas. Another business man added, "If it's more relaxed, then it's easier to form relationships."

executive (회사나 조직의) 간부, 중역   arrange 마련하다   hot spring 온천   impromptu 즉흥적인

업무 회의를 하는 희한한 장소들

아시아의 CEO들은 롤러코스터나 야구장 또는 심지어 감옥과 같은 장소에서 사업을 해왔다. 홍콩 기업의 한 CEO의 말에 의하면 아시아 지역에서 하는 사업에는 사교적 측면이 있다고 한다. 게다가 긴 업무 시간으로 인해 업무 회의는 가끔 이상하긴 하지만 편리한 점도 있는 바, 클럽, 그리고 온천 같은 곳에서 하기도 한다. 이러한 장소에서의 가벼운 대화는 즉흥적인 사업미팅으로 변하기도 한다.

심지어 한국에서는, 자유로운 토론을 유도하기 위해 때로 공식적인 사무실을 떠나 편안한 분위기에서 공식 회의를 가진다. 이러한 장소들은 지극히 평범한 커피 전문점이나 사우나 노래방 같은 문화적인 장소들이다. 한 사업가는 편안한 장소에서는 관계를 형성하기가 더 쉽다고 덧붙였다.

Culture Tip

Depending on the country, business meetings may be held very differently. For example in the U.K. most people arrive five to ten minutes late. Meetings always start with some small talk and are often casual in nature. On the other hand, meetings in the U.S. always start on time, get to the point, and are more aggressive in nature. What are business meetings like in Korea?

*aggressive 적극적인

나라마다 업무 회의는 많이 다르게 진행됩니다. 예를 들어 영국에서는 사람들이 대부분 5분이나 10분 늦게 옵니다. 회의는 늘 약간의 잡담으로 시작되고 사실상 종종 캐주얼한 부분이 있습니다. 반대로 미국의 회의는 언제나 정각에 시작되어 바로 본론으로 들어가고 사실상 더 적극적입니다. 한국의 회의는 어떻습니까?

Idiom Origin

Back to the drawing board   처음부터 다시 하다, 계획을 다시 잡다

"Back to the drawing board" is used when you have to start something over because the original plan failed. The "drawing board" refers to the table where plans and blueprints are usually drawn. By going back to it you're going to plan something over again.

*blueprint 청사진

'Back to the drawing board'는 원래 계획이 실패해서 처음부터 다시 시작해야 할 때 쓰입니다. 'drawing board'란 설계와 청사진이 주로 그려지는 테이블을 가리키는데 여기로 다시 돌아감으로써 무언가를 다시 계획하게 됩니다.

 새 모델이 해외시장에서 인기를 끄는 데 실패했어요.
The new model has failed to catch on overseas.

 흠. 처음부터 다시 시작합시다.
Oh, well. **Back to the drawing board.**

Unit 09 **Personality**

1 제리는 성격이 털털한 것 같던데요.
2 저스틴은 상당히 직선적이죠.
3 그 사람은 뒤끝이 없어요.
4 그 사람 우유부단해요[싱거워요].
5 소피아는 잘난 척하는 것 같아요.
6 젠킨스 씨는 상당히 권위적이에요.
7 크리스틴은 자기 중심적이에요.
8 제이크는 완전 분위기 메이커예요.

1 Jerry seems to be easy-going.
2 Justin is pretty straightforward.
3 He doesn't hold grudges.
4 He is wishy-washy.
5 I think Sophia is stuck-up.
6 Mr. Jenkins is so bossy.
7 Christine is so self-centered.
8 Jake is really the life of the party.

Dialogue Expressions

Complete each dialogue.

1 제리를 만났다면서요. 그 사람 어때요?

I heard you met Jerry. What's he like?

성격이 털털한 것 같던데요.

2 미스터 박은 좀 깐깐한 것 같아요.

Mr. Park seems to be a bit picky.

게다가 상당히 직선적이죠.

3 수잔은 말을 너무 함부로 하는 거 같아요.

Susan speaks without thinking.

그래도 뒤끝은 없어요.

But

4 그 사람은 우리가 말할 때마다 이랬다저랬다 해요.

He always goes back and forth on whatever we talk about.

맞아요. 우유부단한 거 같아요.

I know.

1 He seems to be easy-going.
2 He's also pretty straightforward as well.
3 she doesn't hold grudges.
4 It seems that he is wishy-washy.

5   소피아는 모든 일에 꼬투리를 잡아요.
    Sophia always nitpicks at everything.
    잘난 척하는 것 같아요.

6   미스터 젠킨스는 좀 권위적이에요. 항상 저한테 이래라 저래라 해요.
    He always pushes me around.
    그 사람 눈 밖에 나면 국물도 없어요.
    Get on his bad side and you're a goner.

7   크리스틴은 자기 중심적이에요.

    맞아요. 자기밖에 몰라요.
    You bet. She doesn't care about anybody but herself.

8   제이크는 완전 분위기 메이커예요.

    그래요? 그 사람 말수가 적은 줄 알았는데.
    Really? I thought he wasn't much of a talker.

5 I personally think she's stuck-up.
6 Mr. Jenkins is so bossy.
7 Christine is so self-centered.
8 Jake is really the life of the party.

Dialogue Patterns

Complete each sentence.

A   새로 온 사람하고 일해보니 어때요?
What is it like working with the newcomer?

 좀 욱하는 게 있긴 한데 다른 건 괜찮아요.
He's got a bit of a temper, but otherwise he's okay.

1 관심의 초점이 되어 보니 어때요?
What is it like

2 팀으로 일해보니 어때요?
What is it like

3 그 사람에게 말대꾸해보니 어떻던가요?
What is it like

B 그 사람 너무 건방져서 우리랑은 말도 안해요.
He is **too** arrogant **to** talk to us.

 그래요? 분명히 자기 분수를 모르나 봐요.
Really? Apparently he doesn't know his place.

4 마음이 너무 약해서 거절을 못해요.
He is **too**   **to**

5 성격이 너무 소심해서 여자한테 말도 못 걸어요.
He is **too**   **to**

6 성격이 너무 까다로워서 맞추기 힘들어요.
He is **too**   **to**

1 being the center of attention?
2 working as a team?
3 talking back to him?
4 soft-hearted, say no.
5 timid, talk to girls.
6 picky, satisfy.

Dialogue Strategy

왜 제인은 맨날 나한테 딱딱거리죠?
Why does Jane always snap at me?

전에 말했듯이, 그녀는 모든 사람한테 그래요.
Like I said, she's like that to everybody.

Like I said, 전에 말했듯이,

"Like I said," is used when you want to remind someone of what you said before or want to emphasize it. It is often used when the other person doesn't take your comment seriously or seems to forget about it.

'Like I said,'는 본인이 전에 한 말을 상기시키거나 강조하고자 할 때 사용하는 표현으로 상대가 본인의 말을 진지하게 생각하지 않거나 잊어버린 것처럼 보일 때 자주 사용할 수 있습니다.

DIALOGUE LISTENING

A Listen to the dialogue and complete the sentence.

1 The man and woman are talking about

B Listen again and fill in "T" for true or "F" for false.

2 The woman had a short conversation with the new manager. ( )

3 The woman thinks the new manager is hot-tempered and impatient. ( )

1 the new department manager.
   남자와 여자는 새로 온 부서장에 관해 이야기하고 있다.
2 (T) 여자는 새로 온 부서장과 짧은 대화를 나눴다.
3 (F) 여자는 부서장이 성격이 급하고 참을성이 없다고 생각한다.

STORY LISTENING

A Listen to the article and complete the sentence.

1 The research shows what type of _____ is most effective.

B Listen again and fill in "T" for true or "F" for false.

2 Women preferred lines about general topics. (　)

3 Men were found to prefer pick-up lines. (　)

C Discuss the article by answering the questions below.

4 What type of opening lines do you prefer?

5 What is the worst opening line you have ever heard?

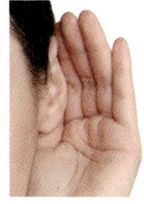 

1 **opening line**
그 연구는 어떤 종류의 대화 첫마디가 가장 효과적인지 보여준다.
2 (T) 여자들은 일반적인 주제에 관한 말을 선호한다.
3 (F) 남자들은 작업 멘트를 하는 것을 더 선호하는 것으로 나타났다.
4 본인은 어떤 종류의 대화 첫마디를 선호하는가?
5 이제까지 들어본 가장 최악의 대화 첫마디는 무엇인가?

Script for Dialogue Listening

Steve Did you meet the new department manager?
Molly I sure did. We even had a brief chat.
Steve Oh, really? What's he like?
Molly He seems like a diligent, reliable person.
Steve That's great. Did you see anything negative?
Molly I didn't get a chance to talk to him for long, so I'm not sure.
Steve I heard he could be somewhat hot-tempered and impatient.
Molly Really? I didn't see any of that when I talked to him.
Steve Did you strike up a conversation with him first?
Molly No, he did. I was too shy to approach him.

department manager 부서장 diligent 근면한 reliable 신뢰할 만한 hot-tempered 성격이 급한 impatient 참을성이 없는 strike up a conversation 대화를 시작하다 approach 접근하다

스티브 새로 온 부서장님 만났어요?
몰리   만났어요. 잠깐 이야기도 했어요.
스티브 아, 정말요? 새 부서장님 어때요?
몰리   성실하고 신뢰감이 가는 분 같아요.
스티브 잘됐네요. 결점은 뭐가 있는 것 같아요?
몰리   오래 얘기할 기회가 없어서 잘 모르겠는데요.
스티브 좀 성격이 급하고 참을성이 없는 것 같다고 들었는데.
몰리   정말요? 이야기하는 동안 전혀 못 느꼈어요.
스티브 먼저 말을 걸었어요?
몰리   아뇨, 그분이 했어요. 나는 부끄럼이 많아서 말을 못 걸었어요.

● SCRIPT FOR STORY LISTENING

Love Advice from Research

Do you get butterflies in your stomach before talking to an attractive stranger? Don't worry because there is a scientific research that will help you start smooth conversations with the opposite sex. One psychologist asked hundreds of respondents to rate how effective different opening lines were when starting a conversation.

The responses were divided depending on gender. Men preferred direct lines such as "Can I buy you a drink?" On the other hand, women liked "get to know you" lines such as "What type of music do you like?" Both genders rejected awkward pick-up lines such as "I lost my phone number. Can I have yours?" In general neither men nor women felt that pick-up lines showed sincerity. With that in mind, make sure the first thing you say is natural sounding and inoffensive.

get butterflies in one's stomach 긴장하다, 조마조마하다   psychologist 심리학자
respondent 응답자   gender 성   awkward 어색한   pick-up line 작업 멘트   sincerity 진실성
inoffensive 마음 상하게 하지 않는

연구에서 얻은 사랑에 대한 조언

　매력적인 사람에게 말을 걸기 전 속이 울렁거리는가? 이성과 부드럽게 대화를 시작하는 데 도움이 될 과학적 연구가 있으니 걱정 마시라. 한 심리학자는 수백 명의 응답자들에게 대화를 시작할 때 쓰는 서로 다른 첫마디 말들이 얼마나 효과적인지에 대한 평가를 부탁했다.

　응답자는 성별에 따라 나뉘어졌다. 남자들은 '한 잔 사도 될까요?'와 같은 직접적인 표현을 선호했다. 한편 여자들은 '어떤 음악 좋아하세요?' 같이 서로를 알아가는 질문을 좋아했다. 남녀 모두 '제 전화 번호를 잊어버렸는데, 그쪽 번호 좀 알려줄 수 있어요?' 같은 어색한 작업 멘트는 선호하지 않았다. 일반적으로 남녀 모두 이러한 작업 멘트는 진심이 결여되어 있다고 느꼈다. 이런 점을 염두에 두고, 처음에 하는 말은 자연스러워야 하고 무례하지 않아야 한다.

Culture Tip

In the United States it is good etiquette to make eye contact with the person you're talking to. If you avoid eye contact, they might think that they are being ignored, or that you are being dishonest. On the other hand, in Korea it is considered rude and disrespectful to make direct eye contact with your superior, especially when you are being reprimanded by them.

*reprimand 질책하다

미국에서는 말하는 사람과 눈을 마주치는 것이 예의입니다. 만일 눈을 피하면 자신이 무시당한다고 생각하거나 상대가 정직하지 않다고 여깁니다. 반대로 한국에서는 특히, 윗사람에게 질책 당할 때 상급자를 똑바로 쳐다보면 무례하고 결례를 범하는 것으로 간주됩니다.

Idiom Origin

Down-to-earth 현실적인

By being "down-to-earth," you are practical and realistic with no illusions or fancy. The earth or ground have an image of being solid and stable, hence the term. "Keep your feet on the ground" has a similar origin. On the other hand, idioms like "up in the air" and "head in the clouds" all imply the opposite, uncertainty and unrealism.

*stable 안정적인 imply 나타내다

'Down-to-earth'하다는 말은 환상이나 상상 같은 것이 없이 실제적이고 현실적이라는 뜻입니다. 땅바닥이나 지면에는 단단하고 안정적인 이미지가 있어서 이런 표현이 생겨난 것이죠. 'Keep your feet on the ground'라는 말도 비슷한 유래를 가지고 있습니다. 한편, 'up in the air(아직 미정인)'와 'head in the clouds(공상)'는 반대 의미로서 불확실하고 비현실적인 것을 나타냅니다.

 새로 온 부사장이 효율적인 생산과 고객만족을 역설했어요.
The new VP stressed efficient production and customer satisfaction.

 그분 정말 현실적인 것 같아요.
He seems really **down-to-earth**.

Unit 10 Drinking

1 제가 따라드릴게요.
2 주량이 어떻게 돼요?
3 스캇은 술주정 정말 심해요.
4 거기서 완전 필름 끊겼어요.
5 대리 운전 불러야겠어요.
6 마지막으로 한 잔만 더 해요.
7 지난밤 술 때문에 숙취가 심해요.
8 오늘 저녁 회식 있어요.

1 Let me pour you a drink.
2 How much are you able to drink?
3 Scott is a mean drunk.
4 I totally blacked out there.
5 I think we should get chauffeur service.
6 Just have one more for the road.
7 I have a terrible hangover from last night.
8 I have a company get-together tonight.

Dialogue Expressions

Complete each dialogue.

1   잔이 비었네요. 제가 따라드릴게요.

   Your glass is empty. _____ sir.

    고마워요. 저도 따라드릴게요.

   Thanks. Let me return the favor.

2   주량이 어떻게 돼요?

   _____

   소주 반 병쯤이요. 전 주량이 약해요.

   About half a bottle of soju. I have very low tolerance.

3   이 술 보니까 도수가 40도예요.

   This drink has 40 percent alcohol content.

   큰일났네. 스캇은 술주정 정말 심한데.

   We're in big trouble. _____

4   이제 술 좀 깼어요?

   Did you finally sober up?

   아니요, 거기서 완전 필름 끊겼어요.

   No, _____

1 Let me pour you a drink
2 How much are you able to drink?
3 Scott is a mean drunk.
4 I totally blacked out there.

104 잉글리시 엑스프레소 주제편

5 대리 운전 불러야겠어요.

벌써 불렀어요. 대리 운전기사가 곧 올 거예요.
I already called. The designated driver should be here any minute.

6 가야겠어요. 아내가 계속 전화를 해서요.
I have to go. My wife keeps calling me.

마지막으로 한 잔만 더 해요.

7 지난밤 술 때문에 숙취가 심해요.

해장국 좀 먹을까요? 좋은 데 아는데.
Why don't you have some hangover soup? I know a good place.

8 생맥주 한 잔 어때요?
How about going out for a draft beer?

미안한데, 오늘 저녁 회식 있어요.
Sorry, but

5 I think we should get chauffeur service.
6 Just have one more for the road.
7 I have a terrible hangover from last night.
8 I have a company get-together tonight.

Dialogue Patterns

Complete each sentence.

A   어제 결국 3차까지 갔어요.
I ended up going for three rounds last night.

 사람들과 어울리는 걸 좋아하시나 봐요.
You sure seem to like to mingle.

1   결국 다 토했어요.
    I ended up

2   결국 병원에 실려갔어요.
    I ended up

3   결국 위스키 5잔이나 마셨죠.
    I ended up

B 술 마시기 싫어서 그러는 게 아니라 술이 너무 독해서 그래요.
It's not that I don't like to drink, **it's just that** this is too strong.

 왜 그래요. 그냥 막걸리잖아요. 괜찮아요.
C'mon. It's just makgeolli. You'll be fine.

4   내가 술이 약한 게 아니라 그 사람이 술이 센 거예요.
    It's not that   **it's just that**

5   그 맛을 싫어하는 게 아니라, 그 술이 너무 순해요.
    It's not that   **it's just that**

6   아픈 게 아니라 좀 어지러워서 그래요.
    It's not that   **it's just that**

1 throwing up.
2 being taken to the hospital.
3 drinking five shots of whiskey.
4 I'm a poor drinker, he's a heavy drinker.
5 I don't like the taste, the drink is too light.
6 I was sick, I felt a little dizzy.

DIALOGUE STRATEGY

 그 사람 술 취하면 어때요?
What's he like when he gets drunk?

우선, 말이 많아져요. 계속 했던 말 또 하고 또 하고 그래요.
First of all, he gets talkative. But he keeps saying things over and over again.

First of all 우선, 무엇보다

"First of all" is usually used when you have quite a few things to say to someone. "First of all" would precede the most important thing you want to say. This phrase usually comes at the beginning of a sentence but can occasionally also come at the end such as "He becomes talkative, first of all." A similar expression is "for starters."

*quite a few 꽤 많은 precede 앞서다

'First of all'은 주로 말할 거리가 여러 개 있을 때 쓰는 말로, 말할 내용 중 가장 중요한 내용 앞에 씁니다. 이 표현은 주로 문두에 오지만 'He becomes talkative, first of all.'처럼 가끔 문장 뒤에 올 수도 있습니다. 유사 표현으로는 'for starters'가 있습니다.

Dialogue Listening

A Listen to the dialogue and complete the sentence.

1 The man and woman are going to have _____ after work.

B Listen again and fill in "T" for true or "F" for false.

2 Elizabeth can hold her liquor. (   )

3 French fries are on sale during happy hour. (   )

1 **some beer**
  남자와 여자는 퇴근 후에 맥주를 마실 것이다.
2 (F) 엘리자베스는 술이 세다.
3 (F) 해피아워에는 감자튀김이 세일이다.

STORY LISTENING

A Listen to the article and complete the sentence.

1 Nick gets drunk by eating meals full of _____

B Listen again and fill in "T" for true or "F" for false.

2 Potatoes and chips were the main causes of Nick's obesity. (   )

3 Nick turned out to be a secret alcoholic. (   )

C Discuss the article by answering the questions below.

4 If it is possible, what specific food would you like to get drunk by eating? Why?

5 What kind of alcohol do you prefer the most?

1 carbohydrates
   Nick은 탄수화물이 많이 든 음식을 먹으면 취한다.
2 (F) 감자와 스낵류는 Nick의 비만의 주요 원인이었다.
3 (F) Nick은 몰래 술을 마시는 알코올 중독자로 밝혀졌다.
4 만약 가능하다면, 어떤 음식을 먹고 취하고 싶은가? 왜 그런가?
5 어느 종류의 술을 가장 선호하는가?

● Script for Dialogue Listening

Sharon   We're finally done with work! Where should we go for some good food and beer?

William   Let's go to Hot Wings Café next door. It's happy hour right now!

Sharon   There are seven of us, so how much beer should we order?

William   I think we need to order three pitchers because Elizabeth drinks a lot.

Sharon   Really? But she gets drunk after a couple of rounds. Remember last time?

William   You're right. She passed out last time.

Sharon   We should just order her a non-alcoholic drink since she has such a low tolerance.

William   I agree. So, what kind of finger food should we get?

Sharon   Chicken wings are on sale during happy hour, so let's get that!

William   Great idea!

be done with ~를 끝내다   tolerance 관용, 내성   finger food 손으로 집어 먹는 음식

섀런   드디어 일을 끝냈어요. 어디 가서 맛있는 음식에 맥주 한 잔 할까요?
윌리엄 옆에 있는 핫윙즈 카페에 가요. 지금 해피아워예요.
섀런   일곱 명인데 맥주를 얼마나 주문해야 해요?
윌리엄 엘리자베스가 많이 마시니까 피처 3잔은 주문해야 할 것 같아요.
섀런   정말요? 하지만 엘리자베스는 두세 잔 마시면 취해요. 지난 번 기억나죠?
윌리엄 맞아요. 지난 번에 완전 뻗었어요.
섀런   엘리자베스는 술이 약하니까 무알코올 음료를 시켜줘야겠어요.
윌리엄 맞아요. 그런데 어떤 핑거푸드를 먹을까요?
섀런   해피아워에 닭날개를 세일하니까 그거 먹어요.
윌리엄 좋은 생각이에요!

SCRIPT FOR STORY LISTENING

Can You Get Drunk Off of Potato Chips?

One British man can get drunk by simply eating potato chips. Nick Hess suffers from a bizarre disease which changes carbohydrates into alcohol. Carbohydrates can be mainly found in grain products such as bread, pasta and potatoes. At first, even his wife and close friends suspected him of being a secret alcoholic. Later after eating a meal heavy in carbohydrates, his blood alcohol level was measured to be the same level as seven shots of whiskey.

Nick is now on a low-carbohydrate diet and is taking medicine to overcome his disease. However, doctors are worried that this rare case will encourage secret alcoholics to blame carbohydrates for their drunken condition.

bizarre 이상한, 기이한   carbohydrate 탄수화물   grain 곡물   suspect 의심하다
alcoholic 알코올 중독자   blame 탓을 하다

감자 칩을 먹고 취할 수 있나요?

한 영국 남자는 감자칩을 먹는 것만으로도 술에 취한다. Nick Hess는 탄수화물을 알코올로 바꾸는 희귀한 질병으로 고통받고 있다. 탄수화물은 주로 빵, 파스타, 감자와 같은 곡식에 있다. 처음엔 심지어 그의 아내와 친한 친구마저도 그가 몰래 술을 마신다고 의심했었다. 나중에 탄수화물이 풍부한 식사를 한 후 혈액 알코올 수치를 재보니 위스키 7잔 마신 것과 같은 수준이었다.

Nick은 현재 탄수화물을 적게 먹고 있고, 병을 극복하기 위해 약물을 복용 중이다. 하지만 의사들은 이러한 드문 경우로 인해 남몰래 술을 먹는 알코올 중독자들이 자신들이 취한 이유를 탄수화물 탓으로 돌릴까 염려하고 있다.

Culture Tip

In Western countries, company get-togethers are often held in pubs. Instead of being seated together at a table, employees usually stand around holding a glass while mingling freely with each other. There is also no pressure to drink, or even to stay for long. What is the get-together atmosphere like in Korea?

*mingle 어울리다

서구권에서는 종종 술집에서 회식이 이루어집니다. 한 테이블에 모든 직원이 둘러앉는 대신 대개 잔을 들고 돌아다니면서 서로 자유롭게 대화를 나눕니다. 술을 억지로 먹게 하거나 오래 있게 하지도 않습니다. 한국의 회식 분위기는 어떤가요?

Idiom Origin

On the wagon 금주 중인

To be "on the wagon" is to abstain from drinking alcohol. The phrase comes from the old expression "on the water wagon" which means that you're drinking water instead of alcohol. On the other hand if you're "off the wagon" it means you are drinking again.

*abstain 삼가다

'On the wagon'이라는 말은 술을 삼가한다는 말입니다. 옛날 표현인 'on the water wagon'에서 온 것으로 이 말은 술이 아니라 물을 마신다는 뜻입니다. 반면에 'off the wagon'은 도로 술을 마신다는 뜻입니다.

 퇴근 후에 맥주 한 잔 할래요?
Would you like a beer after work?

 죄송한데 저 술 끊었어요.
Sorry but I'm **on the wagon**.

Unit 11 SNS

1 페이스북 하세요?
2 카카오톡 들어가 보세요.
3 그녀가 카톡에서 날 차단했어요.
4 리사가 사진 새로 올렸어요.
5 '앵그리버드' 설치 아직 안 했어요?
6 토비의 새 뮤직비디오 조회수가 백만을 찍었어요.
7 전 눈팅만 하고 글은 안 올려요.
8 나도 꼭 가입해야겠어요.

1 Do you use Facebook?
2 Get on KakaoTalk.
3 She blocked me on KakaoTalk!
4 Lisa just posted a new photo.
5 You didn't install *Angry Birds* yet?
6 Toby's new music video hit one million views.
7 I just lurk and never post.
8 I'll make sure to sign up.

Dialogue Expressions

Complete each dialogue.

1   페이스북 하세요? 그러면 저 추가해 주세요.
                                                                          If so, add me.

     미안하지만 전 페이스북 안 하는데요.
     Sorry, I'm not on Facebook.

2   카카오톡 들어가 보세요. 내가 메시지 보냈어요.
                                             I sent you a message.

     잠시만요. 내가 자주 들어가 보질 않아요.
     Hold on. I don't get on very often.

3   그녀가 카톡에서 날 차단했어요.

     차단했는지 어떻게 알아요?
     How can you be so sure?

4   리사가 아기 사진 새로 올렸어요.

     또요? 거의 매일 올리네요.
     Again? They post one almost every day.

Answers

1. Do you use Facebook?
2. Get on KakaoTalk.
3. She blocked me on KakaoTalk!
4. Lisa just posted a new photo of their baby.

5　'앵그리버드' 설치 아직 안 했어요? 최고의 게임인데.
　　You didn't install *Angry Birds* yet? It's the best game.

　　전 게임은 별로라서요.
　　Sorry but I'm not really into games.

6　봤어요? 토비의 새 뮤직비디오 조회수가 백만을 찍었어요.
　　Did you see? Toby's new music video hit one million views.

　　정말요? 제2의 싸이가 되는 건가요?
　　Really? Can he be the next Psy?

7　거기 회원 가입되어 있는 줄 몰랐네요.
　　I didn't know you were a registered member there.

　　전 눈팅만 하고 글은 안 올리니까요.
　　I just lurk and never post.

8　제가 제일 좋아하는 SNS 플랫폼은 인스타그램이에요.
　　My favorite SNS platform is Instagram.

　　정말요? 그럼 나도 꼭 가입해야지.
　　Really? I'll make sure to sign up then.

5　You didn't install *Angry Birds* yet?
6　Toby's new music video hit one million views.
7　I just lurk and never post.
8　I'll make sure to sign up then.

DIALOGUE PATTERNS

Complete each sentence.

A 그녀가 올린 글에 우리가 **돌아가면서** 댓글을 달았어요.
We **took turns** writing comments on her post.

 왜 그렇게 댓글이 많나 했네.
I was wondering why there were so many comments there.

1   우리는 교대로 운전했어요.
    We **took turns**

2   우리는 돌아가며 밥값을 내요.
    We **take turns**

3   모두들 사진을 돌려가며 봤어요.
    Everyone **took turns**

B 'LOL'이 무슨 뜻인지 알아요?
Do you know what "LOL" means?

 그 말을 인터넷에서 찾아보려고 하던 **참이었어요**.
I was just about to google the term.

4   페이스북에 새 글을 올리려던 참이었어요.
    I was just about to

5   그녀의 블로그에 들어가보려던 참이었어요.
    I was just about to

6   카톡하려던 참이었어요.
    I was just about to

1 driving the car.
2 paying for our meals.
3 looking at the picture.
4 post a new entry on my Facebook page.
5 visit her blog.
6 KaTalk you.

Dialogue Strategy

 "친구 추가"가 무슨 말이에요?
What does "friending" mean?

한마디로 말해, SNS에 누군가를 친구로 추가한다는 말이에요.
In short, it means to add someone as a friend on SNS.

In short 한마디로, 요컨대

"In short" is usually used when you want to summarize your previous comment. The comment might have been too long or complicated to understand fully by itself. By saying "in short" you want to emphasize the main point of the comment.

'In short'는 주로 이전에 한 말을 요약하려고 할 때 씁니다. 말한 내용이 너무 길거나 복잡해서 그 자체만으로는 이해하기 힘들 수도 있으니 그 말의 요지를 강조하고 싶을 때 'in short'를 씁니다.

Dialogue Listening

A Listen to the dialogue and complete the sentence.

1 The man and woman are talking about popular _____

B Listen again and fill in "T" for true or "F" for false.

2 The woman used KakaoTalk for the first time when she came to Korea. (   )

3 A picture sharing app is becoming popular in the U.S. (   )

1 messaging apps.
   남자와 여자는 인기있는 메신저앱에 대해 이야기하고 있다.
2 (T) 여자는 한국에 와서 처음 카카오톡을 사용했다.
3 (T) 사진을 공유하는 앱이 미국에서 인기를 얻고 있다.

STORY LISTENING

A Listen to the article and complete the sentence.

1 To get sympathy from visitors posts should contain _____

B Listen again and fill in "T" for true or "F" for false.

2 Some Facebook users get depressed after using Facebook. ( )

3 Social relationships tend to get better the more pictures you post. ( )

C Discuss the article by answering the questions below.

4 How often do you use social media? What platforms do you use?

5 What kind of SNS user do you think you are?

1 useful information.
 방문자의 공감을 얻기 위해서는 포스팅하는 정보가 유용해야 한다.
2 (T) 일부 페이스북 사용자들은 페이스북 이용 후 우울감에 빠진다.
3 (F) 사진을 더 많이 올릴수록 인간관계가 좋아지는 경향이 있다.
4 얼마나 자주 SNS를 사용하는가? 어느 것을 사용하는가?
5 자신은 어떤 종류의 SNS 사용자라고 생각하는가?

● Script for Dialogue Listening

Todd   Do people abroad use KakaoTalk?

Sheila   Not really. I used it for the first time when I came to Korea.

Todd   What messenger apps do Americans use?

Sheila   There are quite a few actually, like WhatsApp, Viber, and Facebook Messenger. Some of my friends also use Line.

Todd   Whoa. I didn't know that there were that many.

Sheila   But now that I have used it, I think Kakao is a pretty good app, even compared to the other ones.

Todd   What other apps are popular in America?

Sheila   A few years ago, Instagram really took off.

Todd   Instagram? How does it work?

Sheila   It's a photo-sharing mobile service. You can upload photos and short videos and share them with other users.

take off 급격히 인기를 얻다, 뜨다   share 공유하다

토드   해외에서도 카카오톡을 쓰나요?

실라   아뇨. 전 한국에 와서 처음 썼어요.

토드   미국사람들은 어떤 메신저앱을 써요?

실라   왓츠앱, 바이버, 페이스북 메신저처럼 꽤 많죠. 제 친구 몇몇은 라인도 써요.

토드   와. 그렇게 많은지 몰랐어요.

실라   그런데 카톡을 써보니까 다른 앱들과 비교해봐도 꽤 괜찮은 앱인 것 같아요.

토드   미국에서 인기있는 앱 또 없어요?

실라   몇 년 전에 인스타그램이 정말 떴죠.

토드   인스타그램요? 어떻게 작동하는 건데요?

실라   사진을 공유하는 모바일 서비스인데요, 사진하고 짧은 동영상을 올려서 다른 사람들과 공유할 수 있어요.

● SCRIPT FOR STORY LISTENING

The Good and Bad Side of SNS

A research team in Germany revealed that 30% of Facebook users feel worse after they use Facebook. Users felt depressed after looking at other users' posts of their holidays and designer items. According to research, posting too many pictures can actually strain social relationships. Baby pictures in particular were so unpopular that apps were made that changed baby pictures to other types of photos.

However, not all pictures made people unhappy. One particular page was constantly updated with photos of cool restaurants that the poster had been to. You would think that this was bragging but the photos always had text accompanying them that detailed the different restaurants and food. Such useful information is very likely to get "Likes" from visitors.

reveal 밝혀내다   designer item 명품   post (웹사이트에 정보나 사진을) 올리다   strain 뒤틀리게 하다
brag 자랑하다   accompanying 동반하는

SNS의 장단점

　　독일의 한 연구팀은 페이스북의 사용자 30퍼센트가 페이스북을 이용한 후 기분이 나빠진다는 것을 알아냈다. 사용자들은 페이스북 친구들의 휴가나 명품 관련 글이 올라온 것을 보고 우울감에 빠졌다. 연구에 따르면, 너무 많은 사진을 올리는 것은 사실상 사회적 관계에 안 좋은 영향을 미친다고 한다. 특히 아기 사진들은 인기가 없어 아기 사진을 다른 사진으로 바꿔주는 어플리케이션까지 생겼다.

　　하지만 모든 사진들이 사람들을 불행하게 하는 것은 아니었다. SNS의 어떤 페이지는 글 게시자가 방문했던 멋진 식당의 사진으로 꾸준히 업데이트되었다. 이러한 것들이 자랑으로 보일 수도 있겠지만, 그 사진에는 항상 설명이 뒤따랐다. 설명에는 식당과 그리고 음식에 대한 자세한 정보가 포함되어 있었다. 이러한 유용한 정보는 방문자로부터 '좋아요'를 얻기가 매우 쉽다.

Culture Tip

When chatting online, the use of Internet acronyms is very common and convenient. These include "brb" (be right back), "gr8" (great), "imho" (in my humble opinion), "j/k" (just kidding), "thx" (thanks) and "wywh" (wish you were here). What Internet acronyms or slangs are popular in Korea?

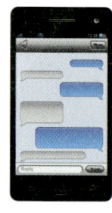

*acronym 약어, 두문자어

온라인 채팅시 인터넷 약어는 매우 흔하고 편리하게 사용됩니다. 여기에는 'brb'(금방 돌아올게), 'gr8'(훌륭해), 'imho'(내 짧은 소견으로는), 'j/k'(그냥 농담), 'thx'(고마워)와 'wywh'(함께 있으면 좋을텐데) 등이 있습니다. 한국에서는 어떤 인터넷 약어나 속어가 많이 쓰이나요?

Idiom Origin

Butter up 아부하다, 기름을 치다

When you "butter someone up", you are praising and flattering someone in order to receive special favors. In ancient India, people threw butter balls at the statues of the gods to seek favor. Moreover, there is a Tibet tradition to carve butter sculptures on New Year's for good luck.

*flatter 아첨하다

'Butter someone up'한다는 것은 특혜를 얻기 위해 누군가를 칭찬하고 비위를 맞춘다는 말입니다. 고대 인도인들은 은총을 구하기 위해 신들의 조각상에 버터볼을 던졌고 또한 티벳에는 새해에 행운을 빌면서 버터 조각품을 만드는 풍습이 있습니다.

 부장님 페이스북에 토니가 댓글 단 것 좀 보세요.
Look at the comment Tony posted on the boss's Facebook page.

 완전 아부하는 거 맞네요.
It looks like he's really **buttering him up.**

Unit 12
Shopping

1 전자제품 매장은 어디죠?
2 손님, 지금 원 플러스 원 행사 중이에요.
3 일시불로 하시겠어요? 아니면 할부로 하시겠어요?
4 따로 계산해주세요.
5 계산이 잘못된 것 같아요.
6 이 물건에 흠집이 있는데, 환불해주셨으면 해요.
7 50%나 할인해서 바지를 충동 구매했어요.
8 그 상품은 지금 떨어졌네요.

1 Where's the electronics store?
2 Miss, we are having a two-for-one sale.
3 Would you like to pay in full or in installments?
4 Split the check, please.
5 I think there's something wrong with the receipt.
6 The product is flawed. I'd like a refund.
7 I bought the pants on impulse as they were 50% off.
8 That item is out of stock.

Dialogue Expressions

Complete each dialogue.

1   전자제품 매장은 어디죠?

    화장품 코너 바로 옆에 있어요.
    It's right next to the cosmetics shop.

2   손님, 지금 원 플러스 원 행사 중인데 좀 둘러보세요.
    Miss, _____ Why don't you take a look?

    아, 마침 잘 됐네요. 10개 선물 포장해줄 수 있어요?
    That was just what I was looking for. Could you gift-wrap ten of them?

3   일시불로 하시겠어요? 아니면 할부로 하시겠어요?

    3개월 무이자 할부 되나요?
    Can I pay in three monthly installments with no interest?

4   따로 계산해주세요.
    _____, please.

    알겠습니다. 이것도 하시는 거예요?
    Yes, ma'am. Are you taking this too?

1   Where's the electronics store?
2   we are having a two-for-one sale.
3   Would you like to pay in full or in installments?
4   Split the check

5   계산이 잘못된 것 같아요. 여기 이건 뭐죠?
    I think _____ What's this here?
    죄송합니다. 같은 품목을 두 번 계산했네요.
    I'm sorry. We charged you double for the same item.

6   이 물건에 흠집이 있는데요. 환불해주셨으면 해요.
    The product is flawed. _____
    영수증 있으십니까?
    Do you have a receipt?

7   50%나 할인해줘서 바지를 충동 구매했어요.
    _____ as they were 50% off.
       반값인 거네요. 그럼 잘 산 거 아닌가요?
    That's half price. Isn't that a good buy?

8   죄송하지만 그 상품은 지금 떨어졌네요.
    Sorry but _____
       흠. 그럼 다음에 다시 올게요.
    Hmm. I'll come back another time.

5   there's something wrong with the receipt.
6   I'd like a refund.
7   I bought the pants on impulse
8   that item is out of stock.

Dialogue Patterns

Complete each sentence.

A

이 가방은 쓰면 쓸수록 멋이 있어요.
The more you use the bag, the more appealing it becomes.

이태리 가죽제품이 왜 좋은지 알겠네요.
That explains why Italian leather products are so good.

1 수제품이 왜 비싼지 알겠네요.
That explains why

2 왜 그것의 기내반입을 금지하는지 알겠네요.
That explains why

3 왜 유통기한이 짧은지 알겠네요.
That explains why

B

몇 퍼센트 할인하는 거죠?
What is the discount rate?

쇼윈도우를 보세요. 30퍼센트 할인이라고 써있어요.
Look at the show window. **It says** 30% sale.

4 원 플러스 원이라고 써있어요.
It says

5 금일 휴무라고 써있어요.
It says

6 출입금지라고 써있어요.
It says

1 handmade goods are so expensive.
2 it is prohibited on the plane.
3 the sell-by date is short.
4 buy one, get one free.
5 closed for the day.
6 off-limits.

DIALOGUE STRATEGY

 설마 또 카드 한도 초과한 건 아니죠?
Don't tell me you maxed out your credit card.

 어쩔 수 없었어요. 너무 많은 물건들을 세일하잖아요.
I couldn't help it. So many things were on sale.

Don't tell me 설마 ~는 아니겠죠?

"Don't tell me" is used usually when you have a suspicion or fear of something and want to know if it's true. Ironically the phrase indicates denial as you are almost ordering someone not to tell what you don't want to hear.

'Don't tell me'는 어떤 것에 대해 의심이나 걱정하는 마음이 들지만 그것의 사실 여부를 알고자 할 때 보통 씁니다. 이 표현은 본인이 듣고 싶지 않은 것을 상대에게 말하지 말아달라고 부탁하기 때문에 반어적으로 부정의 의미를 나타냅니다.

Dialogue Listening

A Listen to the dialogue and complete the sentence.

1 The woman wants to buy _____ for her boyfriend.

B Listen again and fill in "T" for true or "F" for false.

2 The man wants to buy a smartwatch. (   )

3 Designer jeans are on sale at 40% off. (   )

1 a birthday gift
   여자는 남자친구에게 줄 생일선물을 사려고 한다.
2 (F) 남자는 스마트시계를 사려고 한다.
3 (T) 고급 청바지가 40% 할인하고 있다.

Story Listening

A Listen to the article and complete the sentence.

1 Black Friday is one of America's biggest _____

B Listen again and fill in "T" for true or "F" for false.

2 Violence occurs on Black Friday. ( )

3 Black Friday refers to the economic state of stores. ( )

C Discuss the article by answering the questions below.

4 Would you go shopping on Black Friday or would you avoid it altogether?

5 Do you like to shop? Why or why not?

1 shopping days.
  Black Friday는 미국에서 가장 큰 대목이다.
2 (T) Black Friday기간 동안 폭력이 발생한다.
3 (T) Black Friday는 상점의 경제적인 상황을 표현하는 말이다.
4 본인이라면 Black Friday에 쇼핑을 갈 것인가? 또는 이 날은 피할 것인가?
5 쇼핑을 좋아하는가? 왜 또는 왜 아닌가?

● SCRIPT FOR DIALOGUE LISTENING

Fred   What are you going to buy your boyfriend for his birthday?
Emily   I don't know. He's so picky. What do you recommend?
Fred   How about a smartwatch?
Emily   That sounds like it might cost a lot.
Fred   Would you prefer something cheap?
Emily   Well, I only have $100 to spend.
Fred   How about a pair of designer jeans?
Emily   Are they on sale? Why don't we ask the clerk?
Fred   They're 40 percent off.
Emily   What a steal!

recommend 추천하다   cheap 값이 싼   on sale 세일 중인   40 percent off 40% 할인   what a steal 너무 싸다

프레드   남자친구에게 생일 선물로 뭘 사줄 거예요?
에밀리   몰라요. 좀 까다로워서요. 추천한다면 뭐가 있을까요?
프레드   스마트시계는 어때요?
에밀리   그거는 좀 비쌀 것 같은데요.
프레드   저렴한 걸로 원해요?
에밀리   글쎄요, 100 달러밖에 못 써요.
프레드   고급 청바지는 어때요?
에밀리   세일 중인가요? 점원에게 물어 보는 게 어때요?
프레드   40% 할인이에요.
에밀리   정말 싸네요!

Script for Story Listening

The Biggest Shopping Day of the Year

"Black Friday" is the day after Thanksgiving and one of the biggest shopping days in America. It is considered the first shopping day of the Christmas season. Stores often have sales that begin on that day. Black Friday is such a big spending day that it is often thought of as the day retailers finally start to turn in a profit for the year, or "be in the black," hence the term Black Friday.

However, Black Friday is also known for violent incidents. Many involve shoppers getting in fights while trying to get popular items on sale. For example, one woman pepper sprayed people around her who were trying to get the same Xbox game on sale. In another incident, a man was slashed with a knife in a fight with another shopper over a parking space at a Walmart.

retailer 소매상   **in the black** 흑자 상태인   **hence** 이런 이유로   **slash** 칼로 베다

연중 최고의 쇼핑 데이

'Black Friday'는 추수감사절 다음 날이자 미국에서 가장 큰 쇼핑 데이이다. 이 날은 크리스마스 시즌 중 첫 번째 쇼핑데이이다. 상점들은 자주 그날부터 세일을 시작한다. Black Friday는 큰 쇼핑 데이여서 소매업자들이 한 해의 이익을 남기기 시작하는, 즉 '흑자 상태'로 돌아서는 날로 자주 여겨진다. 그래서 Black Friday라고 한다.

그러나 Black Friday는 폭력 사건이 발생하는 것으로도 잘 알려져 있다. 쇼핑객들이 할인 중인 인기상품을 얻기 위한 과정에서 많은 다툼이 발생한다. 한 예로 어느 여성은 세일 중인 Xbox 게임을 사려고 같은 제품을 사려는 사람들에게 후추 스프레이를 뿌렸다. 또한 월마트에서 한 남성은 다른 쇼핑객과 주차공간 문제로 다투다가 칼에 베이는 상해를 입었다.

Culture Tip

At most stores in Korea, the clerks are very attentive to the customers and follow them throughout the store, making themselves immediately available to the customer. However, in the U.S., that kind of customer service is not common, so customers can feel burdened by it. Would you prefer that a clerk follow you around the store?

*attentive 주의 깊은

한국에서는 대부분의 상점에서 점원들은 손님들에게 신경을 많이 쓰는 편으로, 가게에서 손님들을 내내 따라다니면서 손님이 필요로 할 때 즉시 응대할 수 있도록 합니다. 하지만, 미국에서는 그러한 고객 서비스가 일반적이지 않기 때문에 손님들은 부담스러워할 수 있습니다. 여러분은 상점에서 점원이 따라다니는 것을 선호하나요?

Idiom Origin

Pay through the nose 거금을 주고 사다, 바가지 쓰다 (= ripped off)

"Pay through the nose" means to pay an excessive amount for something or to be ripped off. The term originated from Ireland where the "nose tax" was imposed in the 9th century. At the time people who didn't pay the tax had their nose cut, hence the term.

*impose 부과하다

'Pay through the nose'는 어떤 것에 과도한 금액을 지불했거나 바가지를 쓴 것을 의미합니다. 이 표현은 아일랜드에서 유래하였습니다. 9세기에 아일랜드에서 'nose tax'라는 것을 부과했는데 당시 세금을 내지 못하면 코를 베어갔기 때문에 이런 표현이 생겨났습니다.

 300 달러짜리 시계가 고장나 버렸는데 이게 진짜 금도 아니래요!.
My 300 dollar watch is broken, and it wasn't even real gold!

 그럼 바가지 쓴 거네요.
You really **paid through the nose** for it.

Unit 13 Photos

1 실물이 훨씬 더 낫네요.
2 같이 셀카 찍어요.
3 이 사진이 정말 잘 나왔어요.
4 SNS에 사진을 올릴게요.
5 사진이 안 받는 사람들이 있죠.
6 이 사진은 아주 흐릿하게 나왔네요.
7 난 사진 찍히는 걸 싫어해요.
8 왜 그렇게 뒤로 자꾸 가요? 앞으로 좀 와요.

1 She looks so much better in person.
2 Let's take a selfie.
3 The picture came out very well.
4 Let me upload the photos to SNS.
5 Some people don't photograph well.
6 The photo came out pretty blurry.
7 I'm camera-shy.
8 Why do you keep moving back? Come closer.

Dialogue Expressions

Complete each dialogue.

1   이게 줄리아라는 게 믿어져요? 실물이 훨씬 더 낫네요.
    Can you believe this is Julia?

    흠… 제 생각엔 그 반대인 것 같은데요.
    Hmm… I think it's the other way around.

2   같이 셀카 찍어요. 셀카봉도 가져왔어요.
    I even have my selfie stick with me.

    상반신만 나오게 잡아봐요.
    Take it so our upper bodies show.

3   이 사진 정말 잘 나왔어요. 그렇죠?
    Don't you think?

    잠깐만요. 쟈넬이 또 눈감았어요.
    Wait. Janelle closed her eyes again.

4   SNS에 사진을 올릴게요.

    마지막 건 올리지 말아요. 내가 너무 이상하게 나왔어요.
    Don't upload the last one. I look horrendous.

   1 She looks so much better in person.
   2 Let's take a selfie.
   3 The picture came out very well.
   4 Let me upload the photos to SNS.

5   사진 안 받는 사람들이 있죠.

그게 나라니깐요. 사진 좀 잘 받았으면 소원이 없겠네.
That certainly includes me. I wish I was more photogenic.

6   이 사진은 아주 흐릿하게 나왔네요.

그래요. 사진 찍을 때 흔들렸나 봐요.
Yeah, I was probably shaking when I took the picture.

7   자 인증샷 하나 찍죠.
Let's take a proof shot.

미안한데 난 사진 찍히는 걸 싫어해요.
I'm sorry but

8   왜 그렇게 뒤로 자꾸 가요? 앞으로 좀 와요.

그래야 얼굴이 작게 나온다구요.
This is so your face comes out smaller.

Answers

5 Some people don't photograph well.
6 The photo came out pretty blurry.
7 I'm camera-shy.
8 Why do you keep moving back? Come closer.

DIALOGUE PATTERNS

Complete each sentence.

A 그 차림으로 사진 찍을 거예요?
Are you going to take a picture in that outfit?

 사진 올리지만 않으면 상관없어요.
As long as you don't upload the photo, I don't care.

1 뽀샵 처리만 해주면 괜찮아요.
As long as   I don't care.

2 브이자만 그리지 않으면 괜찮아요.
As long as   I don't care.

3 와이파이만 되면 공짜예요.
As long as   it's free.

B 카메라 왜 그래요?
What's wrong with your camera?

 가끔 초점이 안 맞아요. 새 거 하나 사야 할까 봐요.
It sometimes goes out of focus. **I might have to** get a new one.

4 사진을 보정해야 할지도 모르겠어요.
I might have to

5 사진관에 가야 할지도 모르겠어요.
I might have to

6 옷을 갈아입어야 할까 봐요.
I might have to

1 some photoshop editing is done
2 nobody makes the peace sign
3 Wi-Fi works
4 edit the photo.
5 go to a photo studio.
6 change clothes.

Dialogue Strategy

 좀더 붙어요, 사진에 다 안 나와요.
Get closer together. You're not in the photo.

학교 단체사진 찍는 거 같네요.
It's like taking a school picture.

It's like ~ 인 것 같네요

"It's like" is used when you want to compare something with a similar item. The comparison is made so the listener can better understand what the first thing is about or how it looks like. On the other hand, "It seems like" is used when you want to explain a certain action or event in more detail.

'It's like'는 어떤 것을 비슷한 다른 것에 비유할 때 씁니다. 그 비유는 첫 번째 것이 무엇에 관한 것인지 혹은 어떻게 생겼는지를 상대가 더 잘 이해하도록 하기 위해 하는 것입니다. 한편, 'It seems like'는 특정 행동이나 사건을 좀더 자세히 설명하고자 할 때 쓰입니다.

Dialogue Listening

A Listen to the dialogue and complete the sentence.

1 The man and woman are talking about a _____ in the picture.

B Listen again and fill in "T" for true or "F" for false.

2 Angela is photogenic. (　)

3 Angela had nose surgery. (　)

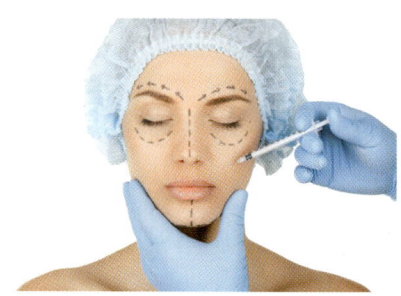

1 new employee
　남자와 여자는 사진 속 신입직원에 대해 이야기하고 있다.
2 (F) 안젤라는 사진을 잘 받는다.
3 (F) 안젤라는 코수술을 받았다.

STORY LISTENING

A Listen to the article and complete the sentence.

1 The "Roaring Lion" was born when Karsh took _____ out of Churchill's mouth.

B Listen again and fill in "T" for true or "F" for false.

2 Churchill's nickname was the British Bulldog because he had a pet dog. (   )

3 Churchill refused to take the portrait due to Karsh's rudeness. (   )

C Discuss the article by answering the questions below.

4 If you had a chance to take a picture of anyone who would it be?

5 What tricks have you used to take a good photo?

1 a cigar
   '포효하는 사자'는 Karsh가 Churchill의 입에서 시가를 빼앗았을 때 탄생했다.
2 (F) Churchill의 별명은 그가 기르던 개 때문에 영국 불독이 되었다.
3 (F) Churchill은 Karsh의 무례함 때문에 사진 찍는 것을 거부했다.
4 어떤 사람의 사진을 찍을 기회가 있다면 누구를 찍을 것인가?
5 좋은 사진을 찍기 위해 어떤 트릭을 사용해 보았는가?

Script for Dialogue Listening

James   Who's this person in the picture?
Emma   She's beautiful, isn't she? That's Angela Park, a new employee in the finance department.
James   She's not very photogenic.
Emma   She looks much better in person. Don't you think she's cute?
James   As long as she has a good personality, I don't care.
Emma   Angela is really a nice person as well.
James   Wait, she doesn't have double eyelids in this picture.
Emma   Oh, right! Maybe she got plastic surgery.
James   I think she looks better in the second picture. I like girls with natural beauty.
Emma   Me too.

employee 직원   **finance department** 경리부, 회계부   **photogenic** 사진이 잘 받는
in person 직접   **double eyelids** 쌍꺼풀   **plastic surgery** 성형수술   **natural beauty** 자연미

제임스	사진 속 이 사람 누구예요?
엠마	예쁘죠? 경리부 신입직원 안젤라 파크예요.
제임스	사진이 잘 안 받네요.
엠마	직접 보면 훨씬 더 예뻐요. 귀엽지 않아요?
제임스	성격만 좋으면 상관 없어요.
엠마	안젤라는 성격도 아주 좋아요.
제임스	그런데 이 사진에는 쌍꺼풀이 없네요.
엠마	오, 맞아요! 성형수술한 거 같은데요.
제임스	저는 두 번째 사진이 더 나은 거 같아요. 저는 자연미가 있는 사람을 좋아해서요.
엠마	저도요.

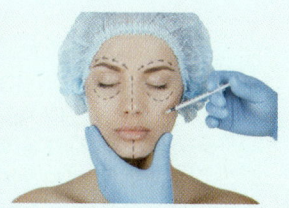

SCRIPT FOR STORY LISTENING

The Story Behind Churchill's Portrait

Winston Churchill's nickname was the "British Bulldog" due to his tough, often harsh, personality. He added to this reputation with his "Roaring Lion" portrait. It was taken by Yousuf Karsh during the prime minister's Canadian visit in the early years of World War II. The nervous young photographer was given only two minutes to take the photo.

When Karsh was about to take the photo, he noticed a problem. Churchill still had his cigar in his mouth. Thinking that the cigar didn't fit the solemn mood of the portrait and atmosphere, Karsh simply walked over and took it out of Churchill's mouth. Angered, Churchill frowned at the camera and an iconic portrait was born. The photo captured the essence of the British spirit, at the time, in the face of war.

harsh 사나운, 가혹한   reputation 명성   roaring 포효하는   portrait 인물사진, 초상화
prime minister 수상   solemn 엄숙한   atmosphere 분위기   frown 얼굴을 찌푸리다   spirit 기상

Churchill 인물사진의 비밀

Winston Churchill의 별명은 '영국 불독'이었는데, 그의 거칠고 때론 사나운 성품 때문이었다. 그는 '포효하는 사자' 인물사진으로 이러한 명성을 더 높였다. 이 사진은 제2차 세계대전 초반 Churchill 수상의 캐나다 방문 기간에 Yousuf Karsh가 찍은 것이다. 긴장한 이 젊은 사진사에게는 사진을 찍는 데 2분만 허용되었다.

Karsh는 사진을 찍으려는 찰나에 문제를 감지했다. Churchill은 여전히 입에 시가를 물고 있었다. 시가가 사진의 엄숙한 분위기와 맞지 않는다고 생각한 Karsh는 Churchill에게 걸어가서 그의 입에 물고 있던 담배를 빼앗았다. 화가 난 Churchill은 카메라 앞에서 얼굴을 찌푸렸고, 상징적인 인물 사진이 탄생하게 되었다. 이 사진은 전쟁에 직면한 당시의 영국의 기상을 잘 나타내 주었다.

Culture Tip

People in America often make hand gestures when taking pictures. The most well known is probably the peace or "V" sign. It became popular in the 1960s when hippies flashed it to propose peace during the Vietnam War. What hand gestures are usually made in Korea?

*flash 휙 내보이다

미국에서 사람들은 사진 찍을 때 자주 손동작을 하는데 가장 많이 알려진 것은 아마 평화를 상징하는 'V' 사인일 것입니다. 히피들이 베트남 전쟁 당시 평화를 제안하기 위해 보여준 1960년대에 'V' 사인은 인기있게 되었습니다. 한국에서는 주로 어떤 손동작을 하나요?

Idiom Origin

Jack of all trades 다재다능한 사람

When you are a "jack of all trades", you are competent in many skills but are master in none. Due to this second meaning, it is sometimes used negatively. In old England jack was a slang term for "man." "Trade" here means skill, hence the term could be translated to "man of all skills."

'Jack of all trades'인 사람은 여러 기술에 능숙하지만 특별히 잘하는 한 가지가 없는 사람입니다. 이 두 번째 의미 때문에 이 표현은 가끔 부정적으로 사용되기도 합니다. 옛날 영국에서는 'jack'은 일반 남자를 가리키는 단어였습니다. 'Trade'는 여기서 기술을 의미하므로 이 표현은 '기술이 많은 사람'으로 번역될 수 있습니다.

 팀은 직업이 요리사인데 어떻게 사진을 이렇게 잘 찍죠?
How does Tim take such good photos when he is a chef by occupation?

 그 사람 정말 **다재다능하죠.**
He sure is a **jack of all trades.**

Unit 14 Dating

1 첫눈에 반했죠.
2 누구 만나는 사람 있어요?
3 안젤라에게 퇴짜 맞았어요.
4 내가 좋은 사람 소개시켜 줄게요.
5 (그녀가) 튕겨요.
6 그녀는 제 취향 아니에요.
7 그 사람 여자 다룰 줄 알아요.
8 그 사람 양다리를 걸치고 있었더라구요!

1 It was love at first sight.
2 Are you seeing someone?
3 I was turned down by Angela.
4 I'll fix you up with a nice girl.
5 She plays hard to get.
6 She is not my cup of tea.
7 He has a way with women.
8 He was two-timing me!

DIALOGUE EXPRESSIONS

 Complete each dialogue.

1 서로 사귄 지 얼마나 됐어요?
   How long have you been going out?

   오늘이 백일째예요. **첫눈에 반했죠.**
   Today is our hundredth day together.

2 누구 만나는 사람 있어요?

   아뇨. 아직 이상형을 기다리는 중이에요.
   No, I'm still waiting for Mr. Right.

3 안젤라에게 작업 걸다 퇴짜 맞았어요.

   내가 얘기 안 했던가? 이미 임자 있어요.
   Didn't I tell you? She's already taken.

4 어제 여자친구한테 차였어요.
   I was dumped by my girlfriend yesterday.

   걱정말아요. **내가 좋은 사람 소개시켜 줄게요.**
   Don't worry.

Answers
1. It was love at first sight.
2. Are you seeing someone?
3. I was turned down by Angela after I hit on her.
4. I'll fix you up with a nice girl.

5　제니와 어떻게 되고 있어요?
　　How is it going with Jenny?

　　힘들어요. 튕기더라구요.
　　It's tough.

6　키미와 썸타는 거 아니었어요?
　　Didn't you flirt with Kimmy?

　　미안한데 제 취향은 아니에요.
　　Sorry but

7　그 사람은 여자 다룰 줄을 알아요.

　　제 생각엔 그 사람 바람둥이예요.
　　In my opinion, he's a playboy.

8　션하고 깨졌어요? 왜요?
　　You broke up with Sean? Why?

　　양다리를 걸치고 있었더라구요. 나쁜 놈!
　　　　　　　　　　　　　　　　The bastard!

　　5　She plays hard to get.
　　6　the girl is not my cup of tea.
　　7　He has a way with women.
　　8　He was two-timing me!

DIALOGUE PATTERNS

Complete each sentence.

A 필립이 수한테 달을 따다 주겠다고 했대요!
Philip said he would bring down the moon for her.

 그렇게 무뚝뚝한 사람이 그런 손발 오글거리는 말을 했을 리 없어요.
There's no way a gruff guy like him would say such a cheesy thing.

1 그런 카사노바가 이상적인 남편감일 리 없는데.
   There's no way

2 스티브가 집까지 바래다 줬을 리 없는데.
   There's no way

3 그런 마초가 여자 핸드백 들어줬을 리 없죠.
   There's no way

B 둘이 맨날 싸우면서 왜 자꾸 만나는 걸까요?
I wonder why they keep seeing each other when they fight all the time.

 극과 극은 서로 통하는 법이죠.
Opposites attract, you know.

4 둘이 왜 헤어졌는지 모르겠어요
   I wonder why

5 내가 왜 그녀에게 그렇게 홀딱 반했는지 모르겠어요.
   I wonder why

6 그 사람은 왜 아내를 두고 바람을 피웠는지 모르겠어요.
   I wonder why

1 a Casanova like him is ideal husband material.
2 Steve saw her to her house.
3 that macho guy carried her handbag.
4 they split up.
5 I had a crush on her so badly.
6 he cheated on his wife.

Dialogue Strategy

🧑 션은 매주 새 여자랑 데이트하는 것 같아요.
Sean seems to date a new girl every week.

🧑 데이트에 관한 한 그 사람 선수예요.
When it comes to dating, he's a player.

When it comes to ~에 관한 한

When you want to talk about a certain topic, you can start out by saying "When it comes to." The phrase is often used when you want to specifically describe a person or thing regarding the topic in question.

특정 주제에 대해 말하고자 할 때 'When it comes to'로 말을 시작할 수 있습니다. 이 표현은 논의 중인 주제와 관련하여 어떤 사람이나 어떤 것에 대해 특별히 기술하고자 할 때 자주 쓰입니다.

Dialogue Listening

A Listen to the dialogue and complete the sentence.

1 Brett and Cindy didn't have _____

B Listen again and fill in "T" for true or "F" for false.

2 Brett and Cindy broke up because he was cheating on her. (　)

3 The man is going to introduce other people to Brett and Cindy. (　)

1 good chemistry.
　브렛과 신디는 서로 잘 안 맞았다.
2 (F) 브렛과 신디는 헤어졌는데 브렛이 바람을 피웠기 때문이다.
3 (T) 남자는 다른 사람들을 브렛과 신디에게 소개시켜 줄 것이다.

STORY LISTENING

A Listen to the article and complete the sentence.

1 Tinder is an _____ app that has gained massive popularity.

B Listen again and fill in "T" for true or "F" for false.

2 Tinder has a unique format which resembles a fun game. (   )

3 Tinder's founder used the app to hire new employees. (   )

C Discuss the article by answering the questions below.

4 Have you ever used an online dating site? How was it?

5 How do you usually find potential dates?

1 online dating
   Tinder는 엄청난 인기를 얻은 온라인 데이팅앱이다.
2 (T) Tinder은 재미있는 게임과 비슷한 독특한 형식을 가지고 있다.
3 (T) Tinder의 설립자는 이 어플리케이션을 사용해 직원을 뽑았다.
4 온라인 데이팅 사이트를 사용해 본 적이 있는가? 어땠는가?
5 본인은 연애 상대를 주로 어떻게 찾는가?

SCRIPT FOR DIALOGUE LISTENING

Annie　　What happened to Brett and Cindy?
Mitch　　They've decided to go their separate ways.
Annie　　How come? They were the cutest couple.
Mitch　　Apparently they just didn't have good chemistry.
Annie　　That's too bad.
Mitch　　Also it didn't help that Brett liked to flirt with other girls.
Annie　　That jerk! Everybody knows Cindy is the jealous type.
Mitch　　Brett would always say that she was too sensitive.
Annie　　I can imagine them fighting over that.
Mitch　　Anyway I'm planning to set both of them up with some of my friends. Can you help me?

separate 따로 떨어진　apparently 듣자[보아]하니　have good chemistry 서로 잘 맞다
flirt 추파를 던지다　jerk 얼간이　jealous 질투하는　sensitive 예민한
set someone up with 소개시켜 주다, 엮어주다

애니　　브렛과 신디한테 무슨 일이 있었던 거예요?
미츠　　서로 딴 길 가기로 했대요.
애니　　어쩌다가요? 정말 귀여운 커플이었는데.
미츠　　보아하니, 서로 잘 안 맞은 거예요.
애니　　정말 안 됐네요.
미츠　　브렛이 다른 여자들과 시시덕댄 게 도움이 안 됐죠.
애니　　멍청이! 신디가 질투가 많다는 건 다 아는데.
미츠　　브렛은 신디가 너무 예민하다고 늘 말했어요.
애니　　둘이서 그것 때문에 싸웠겠네요.
미츠　　아무튼 그 둘 다에게 내 친구들을 소개해 주려고 하는데 도와줄래요?

● SCRIPT FOR STORY LISTENING

Tinder: A New Online Dating Phenomenon

    Tinder is not your typical online dating application. From its inception in 2011, it has been a cultural phenomenon. Tinder targets young people who are tired of writing long and awkward profiles on traditional dating sites. Tinder almost plays like a game. Users can view pictures of nearby matches and swipe right for a "like" and left for a "nope." If two users swipe right for each other, Tinder matches the two for a conversation. With this simple but direct method, Tinder has changed the online dating paradigm.

    Even though, this app might remind you of a game of cards, you shouldn't underestimate its benefits. Co-founder, Sean Rad actually used Tinder to hire employees and even used it to meet his girlfriend!

typical 전형적인 **phenomenon** 현상 **awkward** 어색한
swipe 휘두르다, (카드 등을 단말기에 대고) 읽히다 **underestimate** 과소평가하다

Tinder: 새로운 온라인 데이트 현상

    Tinder는 흔한 온라인 데이팅 어플리케이션이 아니다. 2011년 시작부터, 이 어플리케이션은 문화적 현상이 되었다. Tinder는 전통적인 데이팅 사이트에 어색하고 긴 프로필을 작성하는 것에 대해 지겨움을 느낀 젊은 사람들을 타겟으로 한다. Tinder는 게임 방식과 유사하다. 사용자들은 근처에 살고 있는 상대의 사진을 볼 수 있고, '좋아하기'이면 오른쪽으로 밀고 '건너뛰기'이면 왼쪽으로 밀면 된다. 만일 2명의 사용자가 서로에게 like라고 누르게 되면 Tinder는 이 두 명의 남녀사용자가 대화를 할 수 있도록 해준다. 이렇게 단순하지만 직접적인 방법으로 Tinder는 온라인 데이팅 어플리케이션의 판도를 바꾸어 놓았다.

    비록 Tinder가 카드게임처럼 보일지도 모르지만, Tinder가 가진 장점을 과소평가하지 말아야 한다. 공동 설립자 Sean Rad는 Tinder를 활용해 직원을 채용했고 여자친구도 만나게 되었다.

Culture Tip

Unlike Korea, where potential dates are usually introduced by a mutual friend or relative, the dating scene in the United States is much more casual. Both men and women approach each other for the first time in parties, bars, and even the street to strike up a conversation and ask for a date. How do you usually look for a date?

주로 친구나 친척을 통해 데이트 상대를 소개받는 한국과 달리, 미국의 연애 현장은 훨씬 자유롭습니다. 남자나 여자 모두 파티나 바, 심지어 거리에서 처음으로 만나 서로에게 다가가고 말을 걸고 데이트 신청까지 합니다. 여러분은 어떻게 데이트 상대를 구하나요?

Idiom Origin

Out of one's league 넘볼 대상이 아닌, 급이 다른

When someone is "out of your league," the person is too good for you and you have no chance for a romantic relationship. This expression originates from American baseball which was divided into major and minor leagues. If someone's skills didn't match the league's level, the player was considered to be playing "out of his league."

누군가가 'out of your league'라는 것은 그 사람이 너무 훌륭해서 자신과 연애할 가능성이 없음을 뜻하는 것으로 이 표현은 메이저리그와 마이너리그로 구분되어 있는 미국 야구에서 유래한 것입니다. 선수의 기술이 해당 리그의 수준에 맞지 않으면 그 선수는 'out of his league(수준을 벗어난)' 경기를 한다고 여겨졌습니다.

 마크 좀 봐요. 저 여자한테 작업 걸고 있어요.
Look at Mark. He's making a pass at that girl.

 저 여자 대기업 회장 딸이에요. 급이 다른데.
She's the daughter of the chairman. She's totally **out of his league**.

Unit 15 Lost and Found

1 지갑이 없어졌어요.
2 차 키를 어디다 뒀는지 못 찾겠어요.
3 지하철 선반 위에 얹어두고 그냥 내렸어요.
4 쇼핑백이 어떻게 생겼죠?
5 분실물 센터에 전화해 보세요.
6 언제 마지막으로 봤어요?
7 바로 코 앞에 있었네요.
8 요새 제가 자꾸 깜빡깜빡해요.

1 My purse is gone.
2 I misplaced my car keys.
3 I left it on the rack in the subway.
4 What does the shopping bag look like?
5 Call lost and found.
6 When did you see it last?
7 It was right under my nose.
8 I keep forgetting stuff these days.

Dialogue Expressions

Complete each dialogue.

1   없어진 거 있어요?
    Is there anything missing?

    네. 지갑이 없어졌어요. 분명히 여기다 뒀는데.
    I'm positive I put it here.

2   차 키를 어디다 뒀는지 못 찾겠어요.

    손에 든 거 그건 뭐예요?
    What's that in your hand?

3   배낭 어딨어요?
    Where's your backpack?

    어머나, 지하철 선반 위에 얹어두고 그냥 내렸어요.
    Oh my!

4   쇼핑백이 어떻게 생겼죠?

    검정색 바탕에 가운데 샤넬 로고가 찍혀있어요.
    Well, it's black with a Chanel logo in the middle.

1 Yes, my purse is gone.
2 I misplaced my car keys.
3 I left it on the rack in the subway.
4 What does the shopping bag look like?

5　지하철에서 지갑을 잃어버렸어요. 어떻게 하죠?
I lost my wallet in the subway. What should I do?

분실물 센터에 전화해 보세요.

6　언제 마지막으로 봤어요?

식당에서 마지막으로 쓴 게 기억나니까 아마 거기 있을 거예요.
I remember last using it in the restaurant. Maybe it's there.

7　바로 코 앞에 두고 찾느라 난리를 쳤네요.
I made a fuss trying to find it when

잘 간수해요. 잃어버리면 큰 일 나요.
Take good care of it. If you lose it, you're going to be in big trouble.

8　요새 제가 자꾸 깜빡깜빡해요.

저도 그래요. 전 가끔 차를 어디에 뒀는지 기억을 못한다니까요.
I'm like that too. I sometimes misplace my car.

　5　Call lost and found.
　6　When did you see it last?
　7　it was right under my nose.
　8　I keep forgetting stuff these days.

UNIT 15 Lost and Found

DIALOGUE PATTERNS

Complete each sentence.

A 챙이 넓은 모자예요, 아, 크게 얼룩이 묻어 있어요.
It's a wide-brimmed hat. Oh, it **has** a big stain on it.

 그럼 찾기 어렵지 않겠어요.
Then it shouldn't be too hard to find it.

1   반지 위에 다이아몬드가 박혀 있어요.
    The ring **has**

2   우산에 미키 마우스가 그려져 있어요.
    The umbrella **has**

3   서류 가방 옆쪽에 가죽 손잡이가 달려 있어요.
    The briefcase **has**

B 혹시 내 노트북 못 봤어요? 다 뒤져봐도 없어요.
Have you seen my laptop? I can't find it anywhere.

 나도 마지막으로 본 **지 한참 됐는데요.**
It's been a while since I last saw it myself.

4   얼굴 본 지도 한참 됐네요.
    It's been a while since

5   통화한 지도 한참 됐네요.
    It's been a while since

6   오랜만이네요.
    It's been a while.

1 a diamond on it.
2 Mickey Mouse on it.
3 a leather handle on the side.
4 we met.
5 we talked on the phone.

Dialogue Strategy

일부러 가방을 잃어버린 게 아니잖아요.
I didn't lose my bag on purpose, you know.

내 말은요, 잃어버리지 않게 잘 간수하라고요.
What I'm saying is that you should be more careful with your stuff.

What I'm saying is 내 말은요

You usually say "What I'm saying is" when you want to explain yourself or clarify a previous statement. The phrase is usually used when the listener has misunderstood your previous remarks. To check if the person understood correctly you can say "Do you understand (know) what I'm saying?"

자신의 입장을 해명하거나 이전의 말을 명확히 하고자 할 때 보통 'What I'm saying is'라고 할 수 있습니다. 이 표현은 상대방이 자신이 이전에 한 말을 잘못 이해하고 있을 때 주로 씁니다. 상대방이 본인의 말을 정확히 이해하고 있는지 확인하고자 할 때 'Do you understand (know) what I'm saying?' 이라고 할 수 있습니다.

Dialogue Listening

A Listen to the dialogue and complete the sentence.

1 The man is talking with a woman at

B Listen again and fill in "T" for true or "F" for false.

2 The man probably lost his property in the subway. (　)

3 The man was pickpocketed while he was reading a newspaper. (　)

1 a lost and found center.
남자는 분실물 센터에서 여자와 이야기를 나누고 있다.
2 (T) 남자는 지하철에서 소지품을 잃어버렸을 가능성이 있다.
3 (F) 남자는 신문을 읽다가 소매치기를 당했다.

Story Listening

A Listen to the article and complete the sentence.

1 A three foot long snake was once found on the _____.

B Listen again and fill in "T" for true or "F" for false.

2 Lost items are nearly impossible to find in the Boston subway. (   )

3 Traveling with pets on subways is illegal in Boston. (   )

C Discuss the article by answering the questions below.

4 Have you ever lost anything on the subway before?

5 Should traveling with pets on the subway be allowed?

1 **Boston subway.**
  3피트에 달하는 뱀이 보스턴 지하철에서 발견된 적이 있다.
2 (F) 보스턴 지하철에서는 잃어버린 물건들을 거의 찾기 힘들다.
3 (F) 보스턴에서는 애완동물과 지하철을 타는 것은 불법이다.
4 전에 지하철에서 무언가를 분실해 본 적이 있는가?
5 애완동물과 함께 지하철 타는 것을 허용해야 하는가?

UNIT 15 Lost and Found

● SCRIPT FOR DIALOGUE LISTENING

Terry　　I'd like to report a lost briefcase. It has all my important documents in it.

Rebecca　Do you have any idea where you lost it?

Terry　　I think I left it on the subway. I remember I left it on the rack.

Rebecca　When did you lose it?

Terry　　I lost it on the way to work this morning. I got off at Shindorim Station.

Rebecca　What does it look like?

Terry　　It is dark brown and twice as big as a newspaper.

Rebecca　What brand is it?

Terry　　It's a Samsonite. Do you think you can find it?

Rebecca　Okay. Please leave your phone number. We'll call you as soon as we find your belongings.

report 신고하다　**briefcase** 서류가방　**belongings** 소지품

테리　　　서류가방 분실 신고하려고 하는데요. 중요한 서류들이 거기 다 들어 있어요.
레베카　　어디서 잃어버렸는지 아세요?
테리　　　지하철에 두고 내린 것 같아요. 제 기억으로는 선반에 올려 두었어요.
레베카　　언제 잃어버렸나요?
테리　　　아침에 출근 길에 잃어버렸어요. 신도림역에서 내렸어요.
레베카　　어떻게 생긴 건가요?
테리　　　짙은 갈색에 크기는 신문 두 배만 해요.
레베카　　어떤 브랜드인가요?
테리　　　샘소나이트예요. 찾을 수 있을까요?
레베카　　좋아요. 전화번호를 남겨 주세요. 가방을 찾는 대로 전화 드릴게요.

● SCRIPT FOR STORY LISTENING

The Subway Snake

Have you ever lost anything on the subway? Perhaps an umbrella or shopping bag? Most of the items found at the lost and found are ordinary, but there are some that will blow your mind.

False teeth, dead sharks and human skulls have been discovered on subway trains. One time, a three-foot-long snake was discovered loose in a Boston subway car. The animal apparently escaped from her owner, who was traveling with the snake around her head and escaped to an adjoining car. The snake, named Penelope, was finally caught ten hours later, after the train was taken out of service. Incidentally, this wasn't against the rules. Boston subways allow owners to travel with pets in off-peak hours.

false teeth 의치   skull 두개골   loose (묶인 것이) 풀린   adjoining 인접한, 옆의
take out of service 운행을 중지하다   incidentally 그건 그렇고, 부수적으로
off-peak hours 한산한 시간대

지하철 뱀

　지하철에서 물건을 잃어버린 적이 있는가? 아마 우산이나 쇼핑백 정도일 것이다. 분실물 센터에서 찾은 대부분의 물건은 평범하지만, 당신의 예상을 깰 만한 물건들도 있다.

　의치, 죽은 상어와 사람의 두개골이 지하철에서 발견된 적이 있다. 한번은, 보스턴 지하철에서 길이가 3피트에 달하는 긴 뱀이 발견되었다. 그 뱀은 자신을 머리에 두르고 여행하던 주인으로부터 탈출해, 지하철 옆 칸으로 도망간 것이었다. Penelope라는 이름의 이 뱀은 지하철 운행이 정지된 지 10시간 후에 잡혔다. 여담이지만, 이것이 불법은 아니었다. 보스턴 지하철은 붐비지 않는 시간에 주인이 애완동물과 함께 지하철 타는 것을 허용한다.

Culture Tip

Laws on lost items that you find may vary by state in the U.S. For example, in California, you must make "reasonable and just efforts to find the owner and to restore the property" or otherwise it's considered stealing. What about in Korea? What do you do when you find a lost item such as a mobile phone or wallet?

*restore 돌려주다

미국에서는 습득한 분실물에 대한 법률이 주마다 다를 수 있습니다. 예를 들면, 캘리포니아 주에서는 "주인을 찾아 돌려주려는 합당하고 공정한 노력"을 기울여야 하고, 그렇지 않으면 절도로 간주됩니다. 한국은 어떤가요? 휴대폰이나 지갑 같은 분실물을 주우면 어떻게 하나요?

Idiom Origin

Bark up the wrong tree 헛다리 짚다, 잘못 짚다

"Barking up the wrong tree" means to act on incorrect information or follow a bad course of action. The term comes from hunting dogs which were used to chase animals such as raccoons and barked up a tree if the raccoon went up on it. If the dog loses track and barks up a tree with no raccoon, it would be "barking up the wrong tree."

*chase 추격하다 raccoon 너구리 lose track ~을 놓치다

'Barking up the wrong tree'는 잘못된 정보를 가지고 행동하거나 잘못된 행동 방침을 따른다는 말입니다. 이 표현은 너구리 같은 동물들을 뒤쫓는 데 쓰여 너구리가 나무에 올라가면 그 나무를 보며 짖어대는 사냥개에서 유래한 것입니다. 만약 개가 사냥감을 놓쳐서 너구리가 없는 나무를 보고 짖으면 그것이 'barking up the wrong tree'가 됩니다.

 아까 들렀던 편의점 확인해봤어요?
Did you check the convenience store we stopped at?

 네. 그런데 아무데도 없어요. 잘못 짚은 거 같아요.
Yes, I did, but it was nowhere to be found. **I was barking up the wrong tree.**

Unit 16 Appearance

1 통통한 사람이 제인이고 마른 사람이 켈리예요.
2 저 개그맨 성형 수술했어요.
3 그 여자 양악 수술했어요.
4 그 사람은 30대 후반 같아 보여요.
5 동안이시네요.
6 키는 좀 작지만 비율이 좋아요.
7 저 배우는 어떻게 나이를 안 먹죠?
8 머리가 사방으로 뻗쳤어요.

1 The chubby girl is Jane while the skinny one is Kelly.
2 That comedian got plastic surgery.
3 She got a double-jaw surgery.
4 He looks like he's in his late thirties.
5 You have a baby face.
6 She's a bit short but is well-proportioned.
7 Why doesn't that actress look her age?
8 The hair is sticking out everywhere.

Dialogue Expressions

1   누가 제인이고 누가 켈리예요?
    Who's Jane and who's Kelly?

    통통한 사람이 제인이고 마른 사람이 켈리예요.

2   저 개그맨 성형 수술한 거 같아요.

    확실해요? 여전히 못생겨 보이는데.
    Are you sure? He still looks ugly.

3   '렛미인' 지난 회 봤어요?
    Did you see the last episode of *Let Me In*?

    봤어요. 양악 수술하더니 그 여자 얼굴이 딴판이 되더라구요.
    Yes.

4   그 사람 몇 살인 거 같아요?
    How old do you think he is?

    제 눈엔 30대 후반 같아 보이는데요.

1 The chubby girl is Jane while the skinny one is Kelly.
2 I think that comedian got plastic surgery.
3 Her face is totally different after her double-jaw surgery.
4 He looks like he's in his late thirties to me.

5   동안이시네요.

   그쪽도 나이에 비해 어려 보여요.
   You look younger than your age yourself.

6   샤런 멋지지 않아요?
   Don't you think Sharon is attractive?

   네. 키는 좀 작지만 비율이 좋아요.
   I'll say.

7   저 배우는 어떻게 나이를 안 먹죠? 주름 하나 없어요.
   She has no wrinkles at all.

   아마 보톡스 맞을걸요.
   She probably gets Botox treatment.

8   머리가 왜 그래요? 엉망이잖아요.
   What happened to your hair? It's a mess.

   머리 감고 안 말리고 그냥 잤더니 사방으로 뻗쳤어요.
   I slept without drying my hair. Now

   5 You have a baby face.
   6 She's a bit short but is well-proportioned.
   7 Why doesn't that actress look her age?
   8 it's sticking out everywhere.

UNIT 16 Appearance

Dialogue Patterns

Complete each sentence.

A   어제 라면 먹고 잤어요.
I had ramen last night before bed.

  얼굴 퉁퉁 부을 만하네요.
No wonder your face is so puffy.

1 그가 눈밑에 다크 서클 생길 만하네요.
No wonder

2 그들이 외모지상주의 영향을 받을 만하네요.
No wonder

3 그녀가 머리를 노랗게 염색할 만하네요.
No wonder

B   그 사람은 외모가 특이해요.
He has a unique appearance.

  영화배우 하길 잘 했네요.
It is a good thing he became a film actor.

4 피부 관리 받길 잘 했네요.
(It is a) Good thing

5 그 여자는 쌍꺼풀 수술하길 잘 했네요.
(It is a) Good thing

6 그 사람은 가발 쓰길 잘 했네요.
(It is a) Good thing

1 he got dark circles under his eyes.
2 they were influenced by lookism.
3 she dyed her hair blonde.
4 I got skin care treatment.
5 she got double eyelid surgery.
6 he wore a wig.

Dialogue Strategy

저 여자 코 진짜 아니에요?
That's not her real nose?

정말, 그 여자 코수술했다니까요.
I'm telling you, she had a nose job.

I'm telling you 정말이에요

You say "I'm telling you" when you want to emphasize something that was already said. The phrase is usually used when the listener doesn't believe what you just said and you are trying to convince them that it is indeed true.

이미 말한 어떤 것을 강조하고 싶을 때 'I'm telling you'라고 하는데, 이 표현은 방금 한 말을 상대가 믿으려 하지 않아 그것이 정말 사실임을 확신시키고자 할 때 주로 씁니다.

Dialogue Listening

A Listen to the dialogue and complete the sentence.

1 The man and woman are talking about Catherine and her boyfriend's _____

B Listen again and fill in "T" for true or "F" for false.

2 Catherine recently lost her makeup pouch. (　)

3 The woman fixed Catherine up with her boyfriend. (　)

1 appearance.
　남자와 여자는 캐서린과 남자 친구의 외모에 대해 말하고 있다.
2 (F) 캐서린은 최근 화장품 가방을 잃어버렸다.
3 (F) 여자는 캐서린과 남자 친구의 만남을 주선해줬다.

Story Listening

A Listen to the article and complete the sentence.

1 Huang attacked Chun because he was disappointed by _____

B Listen again and fill in "T" for true or "F" for false.

2 Huang spent lots of money to meet Chun. (   )

3 Chun confessed that it was someone else's photo. (   )

C Discuss the article by answering the questions below.

4 What are some things that you have tried to look better in photos?

5 Have you ever been fooled by an online picture?

1 her looks.
   Huang은 Chun의 외모에 실망해서 Chun을 폭행했다.
2 (T) Huang은 Chun을 만나려고 많은 돈을 썼다.
3 (F) Chun은 그것이 다른 사람 사진이었다고 자백했다.
4 사진이 잘 나오게 하려고 본인이 해본 시도엔 어떤 것이 있는가?
5 온라인 사진에 속은 적이 있는가?

● SCRIPT FOR DIALOGUE LISTENING

Terry   Hey, don't you think Catherine lost a few pounds?
Rebecca   I believe she did. She looks quite thin and has a nice figure now.
Terry   I wonder what her secret is.
Rebecca   I heard she has been doing yoga.
Terry   Really? Now that her hair is shoulder-length, she looks quite attractive.
Rebecca   No wonder she has a boyfriend.
Terry   Catherine has a boyfriend? I didn't know that. What does he look like?
Rebecca   Jeff? Oh, he's 6 feet tall, medium build with fair skin.
Terry   That's a pretty tall guy.
Rebecca   You should see them together. They make the cutest couple.

thin 마른   **medium build** 중간 체격   **fair skin** 흰 피부

테리   캐서린 살 좀 빠진 것 같지 않아요?
레베카   그런 것 같아요. 말라 보이고 몸매도 좋아졌어요.
테리   비결이 뭔지 모르겠네요.
레베카   요즘 요가한다고 들었어요.
테리   정말요? 머리를 어깨까지 기르니까 꽤 매력적으로 보여요.
레베카   남자 친구 생긴 게 당연하죠.
테리   캐서린이 남자 친구가 생겼어요? 몰랐네요. 어떻게 생겼는데요?
레베카   제프요? 키는 6피트이고요, 하얀 피부에 보통 체격이에요.
테리   키가 꽤 크네요.
레베카   같이 있는 걸 봐야 해요. 귀여운 한 쌍이거든요.

• SCRIPT FOR STORY LISTENING

Online Love Gone Wrong

The power of makeup, Photoshop, combined with a flattering angle can even make a non-photogenic person into a goddess. Huang from China experienced this firsthand when he met Chun online. After seeing her picture, Huang spent thousands of dollars to buy a plane ticket and finally meet the love of his life in person.

However, Huang was devastated when he saw her. She was no goddess, but just a woman with a chubby face and coarse skin. Huang, understandably upset, assaulted Chun in public, but fortunately nearby policemen stopped him before it got out of hand. Chun later explained that it was indeed her in the picture and that she had simply edited the photo a little and wore some heavy makeup to look her best.

flattering 돋보이게 하는   goddess 여신   firsthand 실제로, 직접
devastate 엄청난 충격을 주다, 비탄에 빠뜨리다   chubby 통통한   coarse (피부나 천이) 거친
assault 폭행하다   in public 사람들 있는 데서   out of hand 통제할 수 없는

잘못된 온라인 사랑

화장, 포토샵과 얼짱 각도의 결합은 사진이 잘 받지 않는 사람도 여신으로 만들어 줄 수 있다. 중국에 사는 Huang은 그가 Chun을 온라인상으로 만났을 때 이것을 직접 경험했다. 그녀의 사진을 본 후, Huang은 항공권을 사는 데 수천 달러를 써가며 마침내 그의 평생의 사랑을 직접 만났다.

하지만, Huang은 그녀를 만나고는 비탄에 빠졌다. 그녀는 여신이 아니고 거친 피부에 통통한 얼굴을 한 여자일 뿐이었다. 당연히 너무 화가 나서 Huang은 사람들 있는 데서 Chun을 폭행했지만 다행히 주위에 있던 경찰이 문제가 더 커지기 전에 제지했다. Chun은 나중에 그 사진은 자신이 맞고 단지 잘 나오게 하려고 진한 화장을 하고 사진을 좀 수정했을 뿐이라고 설명했다.

Culture Tip

In Korea, a good-looking female face consists of double eyelids, a high nose and a "V" shaped jaw line, like Kim Tae-hee. In the United Sates, high cheekbones, full lips, and wide square jaws are preferred, like Angelina Jolie. What's your personal preference?

*preference 선호

한국에서 예쁜 여자 얼굴은 김태희처럼 쌍꺼풀, 오똑한 코, 그리고 브이라인 턱선으로 이루어지지만 미국에서는 안젤리나 졸리처럼 돌출된 광대뼈, 두툼한 입술, 그리고 넓은 사각턱을 선호합니다. 여러분이 선호하는 얼굴은 어떤가요?

Idiom Origin

Give a cold shoulder 쌀쌀하게 대하다, 냉담한 반응을 보이다

"Giving someone a cold shoulder" means to treat someone unfairly or in an unfriendly way. The phrase originated from an old English custom where a host would signal a guest that it was time to leave by serving a slice of cold meat from a cow or pig's shoulder. Ironically, this polite gesture evolved into the modern colder version of itself.

*evolve 변화하다

'Giving someone a cold shoulder'는 누군가를 부당하게, 쌀쌀맞게 대한다는 의미입니다. 이 표현은 영국의 오래된 풍습에서 유래한 것으로, 집주인은 소나 돼지 어깨 부위의 식은 고기 한 점을 손님에게 내옴으로써 갈 시간이 되었음을 표시하였습니다. 아이러니하게도 이 정중한 신호는 지금의 더 냉정한 형태로 바뀌게 되었습니다.

 애슐리는 매번 나한테 **쌀쌀맞아요.**
Ashley always **gives me the cold shoulder.**

 그래요? 잘 생긴 사람에게는 보통 안 그러는데.
Really? She doesn't usually do that to good-looking people.

Unit 17 Mystery

1 그 사진에 비행접시가 찍혔어요.
2 그것들은 세계 10대 불가사의 중 하나예요.
3 아무도 그 암호를 못 풀었어요.
4 그 이야기가 오늘날까지 전해 내려오고 있어요.
5 언론에서 사건을 조작했어요.
6 전설에 의하면, 그 호수에 괴물이 살고 있대요.
7 다 미신이에요.
8 그들이 뭔가를 감추고 있다는 예감이 들어요.

1 Flying saucers were captured in that photo.
2 They are one of the top ten mysteries of the world.
3 Nobody has been able to crack the secret code.
4 The story has been passed on down to the present day.
5 The media fabricated the event.
6 Legend has it that a monster lives in that lake.
7 It's just a superstition.
8 I have a hunch that they're hiding something.

Dialogue Expressions

Complete each dialogue.

1. 그 사진에 정말 비행접시가 찍혔던데요.

   그 사진 합성된 거예요. 확대해보면 금방 티나요.
   The photo was fabricated. You can see it if you zoom in.

2. 나스카 라인 정말 신기하죠?
   Aren't the Nazca Lines fascinating?

   그게 세계 10대 불가사의에 들어간대요.

3. 전문가들은 그게 암호로 된 메시지라고 보고 있어요.
   Experts think that is a message in secret code.

   맞아요. 지금까지 아무도 그 암호를 못 풀었어요.
   Right. To this day,

4. 머리 없는 기수 이야기 들어봤어요?
   Have you heard the story of the headless horseman?

   그 이야기가 오늘날까지 전해 내려오고 있어요.

1. There really are flying saucers captured in that photo.
2. They are considered one of the top ten mysteries of the world.
3. nobody has been able to crack it.
4. The story has been passed on down to the present day.

5   초자연적 현상 때문에 여객기가 실종된 걸까요?

Do you think the plane went missing due to a supernatural phenomenon?

언론에서 사건을 조작했다는 설이 있어요.

6   전설에 의하면, 그 호수에 괴물이 살고 있대요.

네스 호 괴물처럼 말이에요?

You mean like the Loch Ness Monster?

7   거울에 금이 갔네! 거울 깨면 재수가 없다던데.

The mirror has a crack. I heard that breaking a mirror brings bad luck.

그걸 믿어요? 다 미신이에요.

You believe that?

8   주인이 이상하게 행동하는 거 같지 않아요?

Don't you think our hosts are acting a bit strangely?

우리한테 뭔가를 감추고 있다는 예감이 들어요.

5 There's a rumor that the media fabricated the event.
6 Legend has it that a monster lives in that lake.
7 It's just a superstition.
8 I have a hunch that they're hiding something from us.

DIALOGUE PATTERNS

Complete each sentence.

A

자정만 되면 유령이 나와서 공동묘지를 배회한대요.
A ghost supposedly roams the cemetery around midnight.

모든 게 다 장난일 거예요.
It's likely that the whole thing is just a prank.

1 외계인 소행인 것 같은데요.
   It's likely that

2 정부가 조작했을 가능성이 있어요.
   It's likely that

3 그냥 우연이었을 것 같은데요.
   It's likely that

B

한국에서도 미스터리 서클이 발견되었다는 거 알았어요?
Did you know that mystery circles have been found in Korea?

나중에 서태지 앨범 마케팅이었다는 게 드러났어요.
It turned out that it was a marketing ploy for a Seo Taiji album.

4 그 그림이 가짜였다는 게 드러났어요.
   It turned out that

5 묻혀있는 보물은 없는 것으로 판명났어요.
   It turned out that

6 노아의 방주가 실제로 존재했다는 게 밝혀졌대요.
   It turned out that

Answers

1 aliens did this.
2 the government made this up.
3 it was just a coincidence.
4 the painting was fake.
5 there was no buried treasure.
6 Noah's Ark really existed.

DIALOGUE STRATEGY

그 집에 귀신이 나온다는 소문이 있어요.
There's a rumor that the house is haunted.

누가 뭐래도, 보기 전까진 안 믿어요.
No matter what they say, I won't believe it until I see it.

No matter what 누가 ~해도

"No matter what" is usually used when you have a firm conviction about something. That conviction comes even with contrary circumstances that follow "No matter what." The phrase can also be used by itself as in "I believe him, no matter what."

'No matter what'은 주로 무언가에 대해 강한 확신을 가지고 있을 때 쓰는 표현으로 그 확신의 내용은 'No matter what' 다음의 반대되는 상황과 함께 나옵니다. 이 표현은 'I believe him, no matter what.'처럼 단독으로 쓸 수도 있습니다.

Dialogue Listening

A Listen to the dialogue and complete the sentence.

1 The man thinks the ▓▓▓▓▓▓▓▓▓▓▓ committed the murder.

B Listen again and fill in "T" for true or "F" for false.

2 According to the man the cook is a prime suspect. (   )

3 A kitchen knife was used to kill the heiress. (   )

1 chauffeur
   남자는 운전기사가 살인을 저질렀다고 생각하고 있다.
2 (F) 남자말에 따르면 요리사가 유력한 용의자이다.
3 (T) 상속녀를 살해하는 데 부엌칼이 사용되었다.

Story Listening

A Listen to the article and complete the sentence.

1 The "Taos Hum" is a _____ whose source still hasn't been identified.

B Listen again and fill in "T" for true or "F" for false.

2 The Taos Hum can only be heard by very few people. (   )

3 The Taos Hum can be described as sounding like a diesel engine. (   )

C Discuss the article by answering the questions below.

4 What do you think is the cause of the Taos Hum?

5 What other mysteries have you heard or wondered about?

1 mysterious sound
Taos Hum은 원인이 밝혀지지 않은 미스터리한 소리이다.
2 (T) Taos Hum은 극소수의 사람만이 들을 수 있다.
3 (T) Taos Hum은 디젤 엔진 소리와 비슷하다고 할 수 있다.
4 Taos Hum의 원인은 무엇이라고 생각하는가?
5 자신이 들었거나 궁금했던 미스터리에는 어떤 것이 있는가?

Script for Dialogue Listening

Adam	I think the chauffeur murdered the heiress.
Veronica	He has a good alibi. Also he doesn't have a clear motive.
Adam	Are there no witnesses?
Veronica	None. She stayed at home by herself because she wasn't feeling well.
Adam	I still think the chauffeur is a prime suspect.
Veronica	At least they found the murder weapon.
Adam	Oh? What is it?
Veronica	A bloodied kitchen knife was found outside her window.
Adam	That could be a clue. Maybe the cook did it?
Veronica	There's not enough evidence. Apparently the fingerprints don't match.

chauffeur 운전기사 murder 살인하다 heiress 상속녀 witness 목격자 by oneself 홀로 prime suspect 유력한 용의자 murder weapon 살인도구 clue 단서 fingerprint 지문 match 들어맞다

아담	운전기사가 상속녀를 죽인 것 같은데요.
베로니카	운전기사는 알리바이가 있어요. 게다가 분명한 동기도 없잖아요.
아담	증인도 없어요?
베로니카	없어요. 상속녀는 몸이 안 좋아서 혼자 집에 있었어요.
아담	난 여전히 운전기사가 유력한 용의자 같은데요.
베로니카	그래도 살인도구는 찾아냈어요.
아담	아, 뭔데요?
베로니카	피 묻은 부엌칼이 창문 밖에서 발견됐어요.
아담	그게 단서일 수 있겠네요. 그럼 요리사가 한 짓이에요?
베로니카	증거가 불충분해요. 지문이 안 맞거든요.

● SCRIPT FOR STORY LISTENING

The Taos Hum

Do you hear this sound? [Plays Taos Hum] For decades in America, some residents of Taos, New Mexico, suffered from hearing a scientifically unexplained, mysterious sound. Dubbed the "Taos Hum" due to its humming sound, it was supposedly heard by about 5% of Taos residents. The Hum which has been described as sounding like a distant diesel engine has been reported all over the world. The noise is so disturbing to hearers that three cases of suicide have been reported in the UK.

The cause of the Hum is still a total mystery. A number of countries have assigned research teams to find the cause of the sound but none of their scientific theories have been proven as definite. Due to its mysterious nature, some even believe that the Taos Hum is actually a signal from outer space.

dub 별명을 붙이다   **humming** 웅웅거리는   **supposedly** 추정상, 아마   **distant** 멀리 떨어진
disturbing 충격적인, 불안감을 주는   **suicide** 자살   **assign** (일, 책임을) 맡기다, 배정하다
definite 뚜렷한, 확실한   **outer space** 우주

Taos Hum

이 소리가 들리는가? [Taos Hum 소리 재생] 몇 십 년 동안 미국 New Mexico 주, Taos 시에 사는 몇몇 거주민들은 과학적으로 설명되지 않는 기이한 소리 때문에 고통을 받았다. 웅웅거리는 소리 때문에 Taos Hum이라고 불리는, 그 소리는 Taos 주민의 약 5퍼센트에게만 들린다고 알려져 있다. 멀리서 들리는 디젤 엔진 소리 같은 이 소리는 세계 전역에서 보고되어 왔다. 거슬리는 소리 때문에 영국에서는 3건의 자살이 보고되었다.

이 소리의 원인은 아직도 완전한 미스터리다. 여러 국가들이 이 소리의 원인을 찾기 위해 연구팀을 꾸렸지만 그 어떤 과학적인 이론도 확실하게 증명되지 않았다. 미스터리한 점 때문에 어떤 사람들은 심지어 Taos Hum이 실제로는 우주 밖에서 오는 신호일 거라고 믿고 있다.

> **Culture Tip**

Depending on the country you live in, black cats can be considered either good luck or bad luck. In Japan and the U.K. it is considered good luck for a black cat to cross your path. On the other hand, in the U.S. and other European countries it is believed to be an omen of death and misfortune. What symbolizes good luck and bad luck in Korea?

*omen 징조

나라마다 검은 고양이는 행운으로 여겨지거나 불운으로 여겨집니다. 일본과 영국에서는 검은 고양이가 길을 지나가면 재수가 좋다고 여깁니다. 한편 미국과 다른 유럽 국가에서는 죽음과 불운의 징조라고 믿습니다. 한국에서는 무엇이 행운과 불운을 상징하나요?

> **Idiom Origin**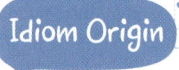

A skeleton in the closet 중요한 비밀, 집안의 비밀

"Having a skeleton in the closet" means to have a shameful secret that you don't want to be revealed. It would be like a murderer hiding the body of his victim in his closet and letting it decay to the point that it becomes a skeleton. The phrase is usually used when the secret is so shameful that if exposed, it would ruin the person in question.

*skeleton 해골

'Having a skeleton in the closet'이란 밝히고 싶지 않은 수치스러운 비밀을 가지고 있다는 걸 의미합니다. 이것은 살인자가 희생자의 시신을 벽장 속에 두어 해골이 될 때까지 숨겨두는 것과 같습니다. 이 표현은 그 비밀이 너무 수치스러운 것이어서, 드러날 경우 문제의 인물을 파멸시킬 수도 있는 상황에서 주로 사용됩니다.

 비밀군사기지 은폐 사건에 대해 들어봤어요?
Have you heard about the secret military base cover-up?

 네. 정부가 **말 못할 비밀**을 갖고 있는 것 같아요.
Of course. I think the government has **a skeleton in its closet.**

Unit 18 Traveling

1 짐 다 쌌어요?
2 2박 3일 있을 거예요.
3 성수기에는 방이 비싸요.
4 오늘 여행 일정 어떻게 되요?
5 서울에도 2층 버스가 있어요?
6 성인 입장료는 25 달러입니다.
7 그곳은 세계문화유산으로 지정되어 있어요.
8 기념품은 어디서 살 수 있죠?

1 Are you finished with your packing?
2 I'm staying for two nights and three days.
3 Rooms are expensive during the peak season.
4 What's the itinerary for today?
5 Are there double-decker buses in Seoul?
6 The admission fee is 25 dollars for adults.
7 It was designated a World Heritage site.
8 Where can we buy souvenirs?

Dialogue Expressions

Complete each dialogue.

1   짐 다 쌌어요?
                 아직요. 세면도구도 가져가야 해요?
                 Not yet. Do I have to bring toiletries?

2   하와이에 얼마나 있을 거예요?
                 How long are you staying in Hawaii?
                 2박 3일 있을 거예요.

3   성수기에는 방이 비싸요.
                 그럼 비수기에 가요.
                 Maybe we should go during the off season.

4   오늘 여행 일정 어떻게 되요?
                 민속촌 관광 갈까요?
                 Why don't we go sightseeing at Korean Folk Village?

Answers

1. Are you finished with your packing?
2. I'm staying for two nights and three days.
3. Rooms are expensive during the peak season.
4. So what's the itinerary for today?

5 　서울에도 2층 버스가 있어요?

그럼요. 그걸 타면 서울의 주요 관광명소를 돌아볼 수 있어요.
Of course. Get on one and you'll see Seoul's major tourist attractions.

6 　성인 입장료는 25 달러입니다.

네, 그럼 몇 시부터 몇 시까지 해요?
Okay. What are your operating hours?

7 　종묘에 대해 아는 거 있어요?
What can you tell us about the Jongmyo shrine?

일단 세계문화유산으로 지정되어 있어요.
For one thing,

8 　기념품은 어디서 살 수 있는지 알려주시겠어요?

이 길 따라 가면 기념품 가게가 나와요.
There's a souvenir store just down the street.

Answers

5 Are there double-decker buses in Seoul?
6 The admission fee is 25 dollars for adults.
7 it was designated a World Heritage site.
8 Can you tell us where we can buy souvenirs?

DIALOGUE PATTERNS

Complete each sentence.

A   그걸 **보니까** 열대섬에 있는 해변이 **연상되네요**.
That **reminds me of** a seashore on a tropical island.

 맞아요. 발리 생각나지 않아요?
You're right. Doesn't it remind you of Bali?

1. 그 역을 보면 절이 연상되요.
   The station **reminds me of** ____
2. 이 곳을 보면 유럽의 성당이 연상되요.
   This place **reminds me of** ____
3. 그 건축물을 보면 피라미드가 연상되요.
   That building **reminds me of** ____

B 동대문 쇼핑타운에 대해 아는 것 있어요?
What do you know about Dongdaemun Shopping Town?

 쇼핑할 거면 가볼 **만해요**.
It's worth visiting if you're going shopping.

4. 시간 있으면 해볼 만해요.
   It's worth ____
5. 줄 서서 기다릴 정도까진 아니에요.
   It's not **worth** ____
6. 목숨 걸 만큼 중요하진 않아요.
   It's not **worth** ____

1. a temple.
2. a European cathedral.
3. a pyramid.
4. trying if you have the time.
5. waiting in line for.
6. risking your life for.

DIALOGUE STRATEGY

 여행 준비 됐어요?
Are you ready for the trip?

 그러고 보니, 여권을 깜빡 잊고 안 가져 왔네.
Come to think of it, I forgot to bring my passport.

Come to think of it 생각해보니, 그러고 보니

"Come to think of it" is usually used at the beginning of a sentence when you remember something or you want to change your opinion about something after thinking more thoroughly about the subject. The second opinion could be totally contrary to the first one or an extension of the first one.

*thoroughly 완전히

'Come to think of it'은 문장 첫머리에 오는데 무엇이 생각나거나 어떤 문제에 대해 좀더 면밀히 생각해본 결과 자신의 의견을 수정하고자 할 때 주로 씁니다. 그 다른 의견은 첫 번째 의견에 완전히 반대되거나 혹은 덧붙이는 말일 수 있습니다.

Dialogue Listening

A Listen to the dialogue and complete the sentence.

1 The man is _____ instead of his friend.

B Listen again and fill in "T" for true or "F" for false.

2 The man had to suddenly cancel his trip due to urgent work. ( )

3 The woman is to go on a separate trip as part of a package tour. ( )

1 making the trip
   남자는 친구 대신 여행을 가기로 했다.
2 (F) 남자는 회사일 때문에 갑자기 여행을 취소해야 했다.
3 (F) 여자는 다른 일정으로 패키지 여행을 갈 예정이다.

Story Listening

A Listen to the article and complete the sentence.

1 In Italy, cappuccinos and caffé lattes are not consumed after _____

B Listen again and fill in "T" for true or "F" for false.

2 Italians usually drink cappuccinos for lunch. ( )

3 Waiters may refuse to bring cappuccinos after meals. ( )

C Discuss the article by answering the questions below.

4 What's the coffee culture like in your country? Is it as strict as Italy's?

5 Do you like coffee? How many cups do you drink a day and when do you drink them?

1 meals.
   이탈리아에서는, 식사 후에 카푸치노와 카페라떼를 마시지 않는다.
2 (F) 이탈리아 사람들은 주로 점심으로 카푸치노를 마신다.
3 (T) 웨이터들은 식사 후에 카푸치노를 서빙하지 않을지도 모른다.
4 여러분 나라의 커피 문화는 어떤가? 이탈리아처럼 엄격한가?
5 커피를 좋아하는가? 하루에 몇 잔이나 마시고, 언제 마시는가?

UNIT 18 Traveling

● SCRIPT FOR DIALOGUE LISTENING

Lisa   I heard you're taking a trip to Europe. I was a little disappointed you didn't invite me to go along.

Max   I'm sorry I didn't let you know. Everything was decided so quickly so I didn't have time to tell you.

Lisa   What happened?

Max   Originally, one of my friends made the reservations to travel but she abruptly had to cancel. She called the travel agency but it was already too late to cancel. So she asked me to go on the trip instead.

Lisa   And then?

Max   I asked my boss if I could take a vacation and he allowed me to go. But there was no other vacancy left on the tour group.

Lisa   Okay, I see. Have a nice trip!

Max   Thanks for understanding.

abruptly 갑자기   vacancy 빈자리

리사   유럽 여행 간다는 얘기 들었어. 같이 가자고 초대 안 해줘서 좀 실망했다구.
맥스   얘기 못해줘서 미안해. 이번 여행이 너무 갑작스럽게 결정돼서 알릴 시간이 없었어.
리사   무슨 일이 있었던 거야?
맥스   원래, 내 친구 중 하나가 이 여행을 예약했는데, 갑자기 취소해야 했어. 그래서 여행사에 전화해보니 취소하기는 이미 너무 늦었더래. 그래서 나한테 자기 대신 이 여행을 가달라고 부탁한 거지.
리사   그래서?
맥스   내가 윗사람한테 휴가를 낼 수 있을지를 물어봤는데, 겨우 떠나도록 허락해줬어. 그런데 그 여행팀에 남은 자리가 없었어.
리사   알았어. 여행 잘 다녀와!
맥스   이해해줘서 고마워.

SCRIPT FOR STORY LISTENING

The Cappuccino Effect

In the West and most places around the world, you can go for a cup of coffee at all hours of the day or night. This attitude, however, will not be accepted in Italy, where certain coffees are often consumed only in the mornings.

One thing you should never do is drink cappuccinos or caffé lattes after mid-morning especially if you don't want to walk around with a "tourist" label on your forehead. These Italian coffee drinks are strictly for mornings because of their high milk content and are not traditionally consumed after meals. Italians believe that the milk in cappuccinos and caffé lattes affects the ability to digest food properly if drunk after lunch or dinner. Tourists, therefore, shouldn't be shocked when a waiter refuses to grant their cappuccino request "for their own health."

forehead 이마 strictly 엄격히 consume 소비하다, 먹다, 마시다
grant a request 요청을 들어주다

카푸치노 효과

서양에서 그리고 세상의 대부분의 곳에서 밤낮에 상관없이 커피를 마시러 갈 수 있다. 하지만 이런 태도가 이탈리아에서는 받아들여지지 않는데, 이탈리아에서 특정 커피는 종종 아침에만 마실 수 있기 때문이다.

당신이 절대 하지 말아야 할 것 중 한 가지는 오전 이후에는 카페라떼나 카푸치노를 마시지 않는 것이다. 특히 이마에 '관광객' 딱지를 붙인 채 다니고 싶지 않다면 말이다. 이런 이탈리아 커피 음료들은 높은 우유 함량 때문에 아침에만 마시고 식후에는 마시지 않는 것이 관습이다. 이탈리아 사람들은 점심이나 저녁 식사 후 이러한 음료를 마시면 카푸치노와 카페라떼에 들어있는 우유가 음식을 적절히 소화시키는 기능에 영향을 미친다고 믿는다. 그러므로 여행자들은 웨이터가 '건강을 위해' 카푸치노 주문을 거절해도 충격 받지 마시길.

Surprisingly, Americans aren't very fond of overseas trips. According to statistics only 30% of Americans even own a passport. That number was even lower before Canada and Mexico required passports for Americans to travel there. Do you like to take overseas trips?

놀랍게도 미국인들은 해외 여행을 아주 좋아하지는 않습니다. 통계자료에 따르면 30퍼센트의 미국인들만이 여권을 가지고 있고, 이 숫자는 미국인들의 캐나다와 멕시코 여행에 여권이 필요해지기 전에는 훨씬 더 낮았다고 합니다. 여러분은 외국 여행을 좋아하나요?

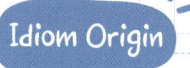

Miss the boat 기회를 놓치다

"Miss the boat" means to miss out on something, especially an important chance or opportunity. In the past, boat rides were very expensive. So when a passenger was late and missed a boat, it was considered to be disastrous, hence the phrase.

'Miss the boat'는 뭔가를, 특히 중요한 기회를 놓치는 것을 의미합니다. 과거에 배를 타는 것은 아주 비쌌습니다. 따라서 승객이 늦어서 배편을 놓치는 것은 손해가 막심한 것으로 간주되었던 것이 이런 표현으로 발전하게 된 것입니다.

 비행기표가 여름 시즌엔 반값이래요.
　　Airplane tickets are half price during the summer season.
 서둘러요. 안 그러면 **기회를 놓칠 거예요.**
　　Hurry up or you'll **miss the boat.**

Unit 19 Food

1 벌써 군침이 도네요.
2 고등어는 비린내 나요.
3 전 음식 안 가려요.
4 국물이 좀 싱거워요.
5 정말 집밥 같아요.
6 김치는 어떻게 발효시켜요?
7 이 콜라는 벌써 김이 다 빠졌어요.
8 저는 단 거 좋아해요.

1 My mouth is already watering.
2 The mackerel smells fishy.
3 I'm not picky about food.
4 The soup is a little bland.
5 It tastes like a home cooked meal.
6 How do you ferment kimchi?
7 This Coke is already flat.
8 I have a sweet tooth.

DIALOGUE EXPRESSIONS

Complete each dialogue.

1. 이 갈비찜 냄새 좋지 않아요?
   Doesn't this steamed galbi smell good?

   벌써 군침 도네요.
   _____

2. 생선구이 먹을까요?
   Should we get some grilled fish?

   고등어는 비린내 나요. 대신 매콤한 거 먹으러 가죠.
   _____ Let's go have some spicy food instead.

3. 산낙지 괜찮겠어요?
   Would raw octopus be okay with you?

   그럼요. 저는 음식 안 가려요.
   Sure. _____

4. 국물이 싱거우면 여기 소금 있어요.
   _____ here's the salt shaker.

   괜찮아요. 전 만두만 건져 먹을 거예요.
   It's okay. I'll just eat the dumplings in the soup.

Answers

1. My mouth is already watering.
2. The mackerel smells fishy.
3. I'm not picky about food at all.
4. If the soup is a little bland,

5 먹고 더 드세요.

   Please have more.

   고마워요. 정말 집밥 같아요.

   Thanks.

6 김치는 어떻게 발효시켜요?

   옛날에는 독에 담아 두었는데 요즘은 김치 냉장고를 써요.

   Long ago, we put it in jars but nowadays we use kimchi refrigerators.

7 이 팝콘 너무 눅눅하고 느끼하지 않아요?

   Isn't this popcorn too stale and greasy?

   맞아요. 그리고 이 콜라는 벌써 김이 다 빠졌어요.

   Right. And

8 샌디는 항상 뭘 먹고 있어요.

   Sandy's always munching on something.

   단 걸 좋아해서 그래요.

   It's because

   5 It tastes like a home cooked meal.
   6 How do you ferment kimchi?
   7 this Coke is already flat.
   8 she has a sweet tooth.

UNIT 19 Food

Dialogue Patterns

Complete each sentence.

 A

 혼자 사는 거 어때요?
What is it like living by yourself?

안 좋죠. 맨날 라면 먹는 거 지겨워요.
Not good. **I'm sick of** eating ramen every day.

1 통조림 식품 먹는 거 지긋지긋해요.
I'm sick of

2 맛없는 국 먹는 거 지겨워요.
I'm sick of

3 아내 잔소리는 이제 신물이 나요.
I'm sick of

 B

 와, 토니는 나보다 떡볶이를 더 잘 먹네요.
Whoa. Tony sure likes tteokbokki, even more than me.

외국인들은 당연히 매운 걸 못 먹는다고 생각했는데.
I took it for granted that that foreigners couldn't eat spicy food.

4 죽은 당연히 아플 때 먹는 거라고 생각했죠.
I took it for granted that

5 두부는 당연히 단백질이 풍부하다고 생각했죠.
I took it for granted that

6 소풍 가는 날은 당연히 김밥 먹는 날이라고 생각했죠.
I took it for granted that

1 eating canned food.
2 eating bland soup.
3 my wife's nagging.
4 you only eat porridge when you're sick.
5 tofu is rich in protein.
6 you eat gimbap on picnics.

DIALOGUE STRATEGY

 김치 만드는 법을 가르쳐주실 수 있을까 해서요.
I was wondering if you could teach me how to make kimchi?

 그럼요. 우선 배추를 소금에 절여두세요.
Of course. First pickle the cabbage in salt.

I was wondering if ~할까 해서요

There are lots of ways to ask a favor. One of them is by starting with "I was wondering if ~ ?" It is a polite way of asking someone to do something for them, without sounding direct or threatening. Shorter variations include, "Could you ~ ?" and "Can you ~ ?"

부탁을 하는 여러 가지 방법이 있는데 그 중 하나가 'I was wondering if ~?'입니다. 누군가에게 너무 직접적이거나 위협적으로 들리지 않게 무엇을 해줄 것을 요청하는 정중한 방법입니다. 더 짧은 표현으로는 'Could you ~?'와 'Can you ~?'가 있습니다.

Dialogue Listening

A Listen to the dialogue and complete the sentence.

1 The man and woman are talking about

B Listen again and fill in "T" for true or "F" for false.

2 The man is going to pay for the woman's lunch. (   )

3 The man and woman are going to have horse meat. (   )

1 what to eat for lunch.
   남자와 여자는 점심 메뉴에 대해서 얘기하고 있다.
2 (T) 남자는 여자의 점심을 사줄 것이다.
3 (F) 남자와 여자는 말고기를 먹을 것이다.

Story Listening

A Listen to the article and complete the sentence.

1 Budaejjigae is also known as "Army Base Stew" due to its

B Listen again and fill in "T" for true or "F" for false.

2 Budaejjigae refers to Korean food eaten on army bases. (   )

3 The name "Uijeongbujjigae" was suggested because it was more accurate. (   )

C Discuss the article by answering the questions below.

4 What Korean dish are you best at making?

5 Do you prefer cooking your own meals or eating out?

1 war origin.
  부대찌개란 이름은 전쟁 시절의 기원 때문에 'Army Base Stew'로도 알려져 있다.
2 (F) 부대찌개는 부대 안에서 먹던 한국 음식을 일컫는 말이다.
3 (F) 의정부찌개라는 이름이 더 정확하기 때문에 이름을 바꾸자고 제안되었다.
4 가장 잘 만드는 한국 음식은 무엇인가?
5 음식을 만들어 먹는 것을 선호하는가? 아니면 외식을 선호하는가?

UNIT 19 Food

● SCRIPT FOR DIALOGUE LISTENING

Nadia	I'm sick and tired of eating at the cafeteria every day.
Jay	Would you like to go out for lunch? It's on me.
Nadia	Sure, thanks!
Jay	What are you in the mood for?
Nadia	Hmm, I want something without too strong a flavor.
Jay	Really? I'd prefer something sweet.
Nadia	Didn't you say that you like Vietnamese pho with chili sauce?
Jay	No, I'm allergic to chili.
Nadia	What about Korean noodles?
Jay	I love Korean cuisine because it's so healthy!
Nadia	Let's go! I'm so hungry that I could eat a horse.

sick and tired of ~에 질린   be in the mood for ~할 기분이 나다
Vietnamese pho 베트남 쌀국수   be allergic to ~에 알레르기가 있다   cuisine 요리
I could eat a horse (너무 배가 고파서) 말 한 마리를 다 먹을 것 같다

나디아	매일 구내식당에서 먹는 데 질렸어요.
제이	점심 먹으러 밖으로 나갈래요? 내가 낼게요.
나디아	물론이죠, 고마워요!
제이	뭐가 당기는데요?
나디아	음, 좀 담백한 게 좋겠는데요.
제이	정말요? 난 단 게 좋은데.
나디아	칠리 소스를 곁들인 베트남 쌀국수를 좋아한다고 하지 않았어요?
제이	아뇨, 칠리에 알레르기가 있어요.
나디아	한국 국수는 어때요?
제이	나 한국요리 엄청 좋아해요. 건강식이거든요.
나디아	가요! 배가 너무 고파서 말 한 마리라도 통째로 먹겠어요.

● SCRIPT FOR STORY LISTENING

The Origin of Budaejjigae

Budaejjigae is a unique dish in that it's a combination of Western and Eastern cuisine. Also called "Army Base Stew," it first originated around the end of the Korean War. As food was scarce at the time, poor Koreans obtained any food they could get from American soldiers who gave them spam, sausages, and canned beans. Creative Koreans in the Uijeongbu area put these ingredients in a deep stew pot along with staple Korean ingredients like red chili paste and kimchi to make the now popular dish.

Since then, any and all ingredients have been added to create various types of budaejjigaes. However, elderly Koreans have stated that the name "budaejjigae" brings negative reminders of Korea's wartime past. Suggestions have been made to change the dish's name to Uijeongbujjigae, for its place of origin, but this has yet to catch on.

combination 조합   cuisine 요리법, 요리   scarce 부족한, 결핍의   obtain 얻다   ingredient 재료
catch on 유행하다, 인기를 얻다

....

부대찌개의 기원

부대찌개는 서양과 동양의 요리를 합쳐 놓았다는 점에서 독특한 음식이다. 'Army Base Stew'라고도 불리는 부대찌개는 한국전쟁 말경부터 처음 먹기 시작했다. 그 시대에는 음식이 귀했기 때문에, 가난한 한국인들은 미국 군인들이 주는 스팸, 소시지, 그리고 캔에 든 콩 등을 얻어 먹었다. 의정부에 사는 창의적인 한국인들은 이러한 재료들을 큰 찌개 냄비에 넣고 주요 한국 요리 재료인 고추장과 김치를 넣어 유명한 이 음식을 만들었다.

그때 이후로 여러 재료가 첨가되면서 다양한 부대찌개가 만들어졌다. 그러나 어르신들은 부대찌개라는 이름이 과거 한국의 전쟁시절을 떠올리게 하는 부정적인 이름이라고 말해 왔다. 이 요리의 원조가 되었던 지역 이름을 따 의정부찌개로 하자는 제안들이 있었지만 아직 인기를 끌지는 못했다.

Culture Tip

In some cultures, it is polite to eat everything at the table as a way to compliment the cook on a well-cooked meal. In other countries, however, it is customary to leave some leftovers or the host will think that you didn't have enough to eat. What is it like in Korea? Is it more polite to eat everything or leave leftovers?

*leftover 남은 음식

어떤 문화에서는 잘 만든 음식에 대해 요리사를 칭찬하는 방법으로 상에 차려진 음식들을 모두 먹는 것이 예의입니다. 하지만 다른 나라에서는 음식을 남기는 것이 관습이라 남기지 않으면 집주인은 손님이 양껏 먹지 못했다고 생각합니다. 한국에서는 어떤가요? 다 먹는 것이 더 예의 바른가요, 아니면 음식을 남기는 것이 예의 바른가요?

Idiom Origin

Get a potbelly   배가 나오다

When you have a "potbelly", you have a noticeably big belly. The word is a combination of "pot" which is a large and round bowl used in cooking and "belly." Hence the word suggests a large, round belly which is a common trait of fat people.

*pot (둥글고 속이 깊은) 냄비, 솥

'Potbelly'가 생겼다는 것은 눈에 띄게 배가 나왔다는 것을 말합니다. 이 단어는 요리할 때 쓰는 크고 둥그런 그릇의 'pot'과 'belly'의 합성어로 뚱뚱한 사람들의 공통적인 특징인 크고 둥그런 배를 암시하고 있습니다.

 오랜만이네. 언제 그렇게 **배가 나온 거야?**
I haven't seen you in years. When did you **get a potbelly**?

 요즘 맥주를 엄청 먹었거든.
I've been drinking a lot of beer lately.

Unit 20 Sports

1 3:3 동점이에요.
2 그 선수가 만루홈런을 쳤어요.
3 두 선수가 막상막하로 골인했어요.
4 저 사람 신인 선수 아니에요?
5 상대팀이 후반전에 한 골 넣었어요.
6 그쪽 스타 선수가 반칙했어요.
7 어느 팀 응원하세요?
8 결승전이 무승부로 끝나버렸어요.

1 It is tied at three to three.
2 He hit a grand slam.
3 The two runners finished the race neck and neck.
4 Isn't that the new rookie?
5 The other team scored a goal in the second half.
6 Their star player made a foul.
7 Which team are you rooting for?
8 The championship game just ended in a draw.

Dialogue Expressions

Complete each dialogue.

1 누가 이기고 있어요?
   Who's winning the game?

   3:3 동점이에요. 연장전 가겠어요.
   _____ This might go into overtime.

2 4번 타자 나오네요.
   Here comes the cleanup hitter for us.

   만루홈런 한번 쳐주면 좋겠어요. 지금 딱 필요한데.
   _____ We really need it.

3 그 두 선수는 막상막하로 골인했어요.
   _____

   휴. 정말 아슬아슬했어요.
   Whew. That was a close race.

4 저 사람 신인 선수 아니에요? 내야수예요, 외야수예요?
   _____ Is he an infielder or an outfielder?

   실은 포수예요.
   He's a catcher actually.

1 It is tied at three to three.
2 I hope he hits a grand slam.
3 The two runners finished the race neck and neck.
4 Isn't that the new rookie?

5   상대팀이 후반전에 한 골 넣었어요.

아. 우리 지고 있는 거네요. 시간 다 돼가는데.
Oh. We are losing now and time is running out.

6   그쪽 스타 선수가 반칙했어요.

진짜요? 퇴장당할지도 모르겠네요.
Really? Maybe he will be kicked out of the game.

7   어느 팀 응원하세요?

타이거즈요, 근데 벌써 9회말이에요.
The Tigers, but it's already the bottom of the 9th inning.

8   결승전이 무승부로 끝나버렸어요.

승부차기로 결정하겠군요. 못 보겠어요.
It's going to be settled by a shootout. I can't watch.

5   The other team scored a goal in the second half.
6   Their star player just made a foul.
7   Which team are you rooting for?
8   The championship game just ended in a draw.

DIALOGUE PATTERNS

Complete each sentence.

A 비오면 어떡하죠?
What if it rains?

 그럼 수중전이 되는 거죠.
Then the match will be played on a wet field.

1 부상당하면 어떡하죠?
   What if

2 승부차기에서 지면 어떡하죠?
   What if

3 일이 잘못되면 어떡해요?
   What if

B 원정 경기라 걱정되네요.
I'm worried since it's a road game.

 홈경기나 원정경기나 **상관 없어요**.
It doesn't matter if we are at home or away.

4 다른 구단과 계약해도 상관없어요.
   It doesn't matter if

5 정상급 투수라고 해도 상관없어요.
   It doesn't matter if

6 연장전까지 가도 상관없어요.
   It doesn't matter whether

1 he gets injured?
2 we lose in the penalty shootout?
3 something goes wrong?
4 he signs with another team.
5 he's a top-notch pitcher.
6 the game goes to overtime.

DIALOGUE STRATEGY

 왜 우리가 졌다고 생각하세요?
Why do you think we lost?

 내가 보기엔, 상대팀은 더 좋은 선수들이 있었거든요.
They way I see it, the opposing team just had better athletes.

The way I see it 내가 보기엔

To express an opinion in a respectful way, you can start out by saying "The way I see it." The phrase is often used when there is a difference of opinion with another person. By saying "The way I see it" you can share your views without sounding offensive.

*offensive 불쾌한, 공격적인

정중하게 의견을 표현하고 싶을 때 'The way I see it'으로 말을 시작할 수 있습니다. 이 표현은 다른 사람과 의견 차이가 있을 때 주로 사용되는데 'The way I see it'이라고 말함으로써 공격적인 느낌을 주지 않으면서 생각을 공유할 수 있습니다.

Dialogue Listening

A Listen to the dialogue and complete the sentence.

1 The Korean team ended up going to the _____

B Listen again and fill in "T" for true or "F" for false.

2 The game ended in a draw. (   )

3 The man bet on the game. (   )

1 semifinals.
한국팀이 결국 준결승에 진출하게 되었다.
2 (F) 시합은 동점으로 끝났다.
3 (T) 남자는 시합에 내기를 했다.

Story Listening

A Listen to the article and complete the sentence.

1 Many people watch the Super Bowl for its _____ rather than the game itself.

B Listen again and fill in "T" for true or "F" for false.

2 Due to strict regulations Super Bowl commercials are hard to make. ( )

3 Koreans are known to watch the Super Bowl for its commercials. ( )

C Discuss the article by answering the questions below.

4 Do you believe that spending big on Super Bowl commercials is a wise investment?

5 When you watch sports, where and with whom do you watch them?

1 commercials
 많은 사람들이 경기보다 광고 때문에 수퍼볼을 시청한다.
2 (F) 엄격한 규정 때문에 수퍼볼 광고는 만들기 어렵다.
3 (F) 한국 사람들이 광고 때문에 수퍼볼을 본다고 알려져 있다.
4 수퍼볼에 막대한 돈을 쓰는 것이 현명한 투자라고 생각하는가?
5 스포츠를 볼 때 어디서 누구와 보는가?

SCRIPT FOR DIALOGUE LISTENING

Jessica   Who's playing?

Matthew   It's Korea versus Japan. The winning team will advance to the semifinals.

Jessica   What's the score?

Matthew   We're tied at 2-2. I hope it doesn't end in a draw.

Jessica   Who scored for the Korean team?

Matthew   Ki Sung-yong scored the first goal and Son Heung-min scored the second.

Jessica   Which team are you rooting for?

Matthew   I'm rooting for Korea of course.

Jessica   We got another goal! We won!

Matthew   And I won a free lunch from Mark!

advance 진출하다, 진전을 보다   semifinal 준결승   score 득점, 득점하다   be tied 동점인
end in a draw 동점으로 끝나다   root for ~을 응원하다

제시카   누구 경기예요?
매튜   한국 대 일본이요. 이기는 팀이 준결승전에 진출해요.
제시카   스코어는 어떻게 돼요?
매튜   2 대 2로 동점이에요. 동점으로 끝나지 않기를 바래야죠.
제시카   한국팀에서는 누가 골을 넣었어요?
매튜   기성용이 첫 골을 넣었고, 손흥민이 두 번째 골을 넣었어요.
제시카   어느 팀을 응원해요?
매튜   당연히 한국을 응원하죠.
제시카   우리가 또 골을 넣었어요. 우리가 이겼어요!
매튜   그리고 난 마크한테 공짜 점심을 땄네요!

● SCRIPT FOR STORY LISTENING

Super Bowl Commercials

The Super Bowl is the championship game in American football and is watched by 114 million people around the world. However, the Super Bowl is perhaps best known for its TV commercials. According to a survey, 50% of the people who watch the game watch it only for the commercials. Super Bowl commercials are almost always eye-catching with their high level of humor and shock effect.

Super Bowl commercials often feature expensive special effects, "A list" actors, and abundant humor. A 30-second ad usually costs $1 million to $3 million to make and $4.5 million to air. Three regular spenders on Super Bowl commercials happen to be Korean firms: Samsung (smartphones), Hyundai (cars), and Kia (cars). Kia in particular has aired commercials for six straight Super Bowls.

championship game 결승전   commercial 광고   eye-catching 시선을 잡아 끄는
feature ~을 특징으로 한다   special effect 특수효과

수퍼볼 광고

수퍼볼은 미식축구 결승전이며 세계적으로 1억 천 4백만 명이 시청한다. 하지만 아마도 수퍼볼은 텔레비전 광고 때문에 제일 많이 알려져 있을 것이다. 설문조사에 따르면 이 경기 시청자의 50퍼센트가 오직 광고 때문에 이 경기를 본다고 한다. 수퍼볼 광고는 거의 항상 고품격 유머와 충격 효과로 시선을 끈다.

수퍼볼 광고는 비싼 특수효과와 A급 배우, 풍부한 유머가 특징이다. 30초짜리 광고 제작에 1백만 달러에서 3백만 달러까지 비용이 들고 방송하는 데는 4백 5십만 달러가 소요된다. 수퍼볼 광고의 단골 고객사 세 군데는 한국 회사들이다: 삼성(스마트폰), 현대(자동차), 기아(자동차)이다. 특히 기아는 여섯 번 연속 수퍼볼 광고를 했다.

Culture Tip

For most Americans trips to the baseball ballpark don't feel complete without a hot dog from the concession stand. Hot dogs, which are sausages on buns, have been a part of American baseball for more than a century. Other popular snacks are peanuts, nachos and ice cream. What snacks are sold at your local stadium?

*concession stand 매점

미국인 대부분은 야구장 갈 때 매점에서 파는 핫도그가 없으면 뭔가 빠졌다고 생각합니다. 둥그런 빵 위에 얹은 소시지인 핫도그는 100년이 넘도록 미국 야구의 일부였습니다. 그 외 인기 있는 간식은 땅콩, 나초 그리고 아이스크림입니다. 여러분이 사는 지역 경기장에서는 어떤 스낵들을 판매하나요?

Idiom Origin

Ballpark figure 대략적인 수치

"Ballpark figure" which means a rough estimate or approximation predictably comes from baseball. Baseball parks while spacious were always enclosed spaces. Therefore, "ballpark figures" while rough still had to be within reasonable range of the actual figure.

*rough estimate 대략적인 추산 approximation 근사치 enclosed (담 등으로) 에워싸인

대략적인 추산이나 근사치를 의미하는 'ballpark figure'는 예상대로 야구에서 유래한 것입니다. 야구장은 넓긴 하지만 담장으로 둘러싸인 곳이어서 'ballpark figure'는 대략적이긴 하지만 실제 수치로부터 합리적인 범위 안에 있어야 하는 것이죠.

 지난 달 매출은 어땠어요?
How were sales last month?

 정확한 숫자는 몰라요. 대략적인 수치만 알려줄 수 있어요.
I don't have the exact numbers. I can only give you a **ballpark figure**.

ENGLISH EXPRESSO

 ENGLISH EXPRESSO

21세기 외국어 교육의 선두주자

하이잉글리쉬는 기업 출강, 대학 교육, 온라인 교육을 전문으로 하는 외국어 교육 기업으로서 엄격한 강사 선발 기준과 체계적인 학사 관리로 최상의 교육 서비스를 제공합니다.

1 기업 출강

교육담당자를 전담 배치하는 체계적인 관리 시스템으로 높은 출석률과 최고의 만족도를 자랑합니다.

2 연수원 합숙 교육

회사에서 선발된 학습자들을 대상으로 다양하고 심도있는 활동을 집중적으로 다루어 실력 향상도가 매우 높습니다. 또한 교육외 시간의 체험 활동을 통하여 모국어 수준의 언어습득 효과를 낼 수 있습니다.

3 전화 / 화상 외국어 교육

실시간 쌍방향 전화 / 동영상 강의로, 수업 중 학습자가 질문하는 내용에 대해 강사가 실시간으로 생생하게 답변하며, 학습자는 강의 내용을 바로 확인할 수 있습니다.

4 온라인 교육

다년간의 기업 외국어 출강 경험과 300여 명의 전문 강사들의 다양한 외국어, 동영상 강좌를 제공합니다.

5 말하기 시험 TOSEB

2004년 자체 개발한 비즈니스 말하기 능력 테스트로 원어민 면접관과 10분 전화 회화로 레벨 평가하는 것으로 자기소개, 일상회화, 업무 대화로 영역별 녹취파일 및 평가표를 제공하고 있습니다.

6 대학 외국어 교육

취업 영어 면접, 영문 이력서 특강, 외국계기업 및 국제기구 인사담당자 초청 특강, 취업대비, 학기제 수업, 해외 인턴십 강의를 진행합니다.

 하이잉글리쉬　www.hienglish.com　Tel : 02-335-1002　Email : market1@hienglish.com

HiChinese

기업 출강 NO.1 파트너 하이차이니즈가 중국과 同行하는 길을 열어 드립니다!

잘 한다
Hi Chinese
1등 노하우

믿을 수 있다

중국 명문 복단대
언어교육원 프로그램

체계적이다
Hi-Five LEARNING
MANAGEMENT SYSTEM
온라인 학사관리
시스템

전문적이다
기업연수원
중국어 집중과정
(삼성, LG, SK, 한화)

중국어 출강 교육
임원 1:1 교육

전화 중국어
1:1 중국어 교육

중국어 통번역
VIP수행통역
이메일 문서 번역

중국 현지 연수
연수원 집중과정

중국 문화 특강
China Academy

중국어 면접
에세이 평가

B2B 중국어 교육 전문 **하이차이니즈**가
임직원 **中国通** 양성을 위해
고객을 모시겠습니다.

 하이차이니즈 www.hichinese.co.kr   Tel: 1688-8096   Email: service@hichinese.co.k

www.hicalling.co.kr

비즈니스 회화 과정
비즈니스 업무수행 시 필요한 외국어 능력 증대

기초 일반 회화 과정
Free Talking 형식의 1:1 수업

각종 시험대비 과정
SPA / OPIC / TOEIC SPEAKING 과정 연습

개인별 맞춤 교육
사전 상담 및 스케줄 조정 가능
철저한 피드백 및 사후 관리

 하이콜링 www.hicalling.co.kr Tel : 070-8730-5961 Email : hicalling2@hienglish.com

세상에서 가장 간편한 해외여행

HiCafe는 부담 없는 가격으로 좋은 사람들과 외국어를 즐기는 문화 공간입니다.

스터디룸 이용 안내

주중 : 시간당 1,500원

주말 : 시간당 3,000원

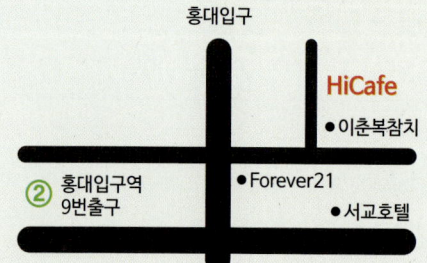

홍대입구
HiCafe
● 이춘복참치
② 홍대입구역 9번출구
● Forever21
● 서교호텔

HiCafe

	open	close
Sun~Thu	11:30am ~ 11:00pm	
Fri~Sat	11:30am ~ 01:00am	

Tel : 070-8730-1697
Add : 서울시 마포구 홍익로5안길 8
Web : www.hicafe.co.kr

 무료 MP3 다운로드
www.hienglish.com

 모바일 스트리밍
m.hienglish.com

 팟캐스트
www.podbbang.com

국내 896개 대기업이 채택한 비즈니스 영어 교재

비즈니스 잉글리시 케첩
Business English Catch-up

비즈니스 잉글리시 케첩 시리즈는 오늘의 글로벌 시대에 필요한 커뮤니케이션 능력을 향상시킬 수 있도록 제작한 교재이다. 다양한 비즈니스 환경에서 외국인 파트너의 영어 실력을 케첩(catch-up)하고 자신있게 협력하고 의사소통할 수 있도록 실무에 자주 사용하는 표현과 어휘 중심으로 구성하였으며 읽고, 듣고, 쓰고 말하는 기회를 제공한다.

Negotiation
Negotiation 편은 협상 영어에 중점을 둔 책으로 배경조사부터 계약 체결까지 협상의 모든 단계를 다룬다.

· 저자: 윤주영　· 출간일: 2015년 7월 1일　· 페이지: 192쪽　· 가격: 20,000원

Presentation
Presentation 편은 다양한 프레젠테이션을 영어로 매끄럽게 진행하는 데 필요한 발표 전략과 핵심 표현을 실은 책이다.

· 저자: 윤주영　· 출간일: 2015년 7월 1일　· 페이지: 192쪽　· 가격: 20,000원

Meeting
Meeting 편은 외국 파트너들과 회의를 진행할 때 나타날 수 있는 각 시나리오를 다룬다.

· 저자: 윤주영　· 출간일: 2015년 7월 1일　· 페이지: 192쪽　· 가격: 20,000원

Telephoning
Telephoning 편은 주문부터 약속을 잡는 것까지 전화 영어와 관련하여 다양한 상황을 다룬다.

· 저자: 윤주영　· 출간일: 2015년 7월 1일　· 페이지: 192쪽　· 가격: 20,000원

Email
Email 편은 직장에서 자주 쓰는 이메일, 회의록, 계약서 작성법을 다루고 있다.

· 저자: 윤주영　· 출간일: 2015년 7월 1일　· 페이지: 288쪽　· 가격: 20,000원

[바로 통하는, SPA 이렇게 준비하라!]

본 책은 SPA 시험의 문제 유형이나 시험 진행방식을 철저히 분석해 실제 시험의 흐름을 정확히 반영하였다. 이에 더하여 문제 유형에 대한 해설과 고득점 획득 전략도 자세히 소개하고 있다. 시험 유형 학습이 끝나면 15세트의 실전문제를 통해 충분한 최종 리허설도 가능하다. 모든 질문을 듣고 연습할 수 있도록 MP3 파일이 제공된다.

이 책은 현대·기아자동차 그룹의 영어 면접시험인 SPA(Speaking Proficiency Assessment)를 위한 가이드북이다. 현대 그룹은 OPIc이나 TOEIC Speaking 같은 다른 영어 스피킹 성적을 인정하지 않기 때문에 SPA 시험은 그룹의 임직원이나 입사 희망자들이라면 반드시 준비해야 한다.

저자 : HiEnglish R&D   출간일 : 2014년 6월 2일
가격 : 20,000원   220쪽 | 190*260*12mm

책 구매 시 SPA 모의테스트 **50% 할인!**

현장테스트 : ~~60,000원~~ ➔ **30,000원** / 전화테스트 : ~~50,000원~~ ➔ **25,000원**

신청 방법 하이잉글리쉬 홈페이지(www.hienglish.com)에서 신청
할인 적용 방법 영수증 사진 전송 시 코드번호 제공
문의 070-7826-0865, editor1@hienglish.com